Mapping Queerness in Times of Uncertainty

This book offers a new critical perspective on emerging and alternative 'spaces' for emancipation within lesbian, gay, bisexual, transgender, and queer (LGBTQ) communities. It considers these across various geographic regions, and in times of social, political, and ecological uncertainty and change. The work delves into complex, often invisible spaces where queer communities navigate social, political, and ecological upheavals. Through a blend of critical theory, digital mapping, and rich case studies from regions like the Middle East, North Africa, Singapore, Poland, and Russia, the authors illuminate the intersecting challenges of neocolonial legacies, religious conservatism, and political repression.

A must-read for scholars and advocates involved with human rights and LGBTQ organizations; this book provides a nuanced, interdisciplinary perspective on the evolving landscapes of queer emancipation and resistance. As such, it will appeal to scholars and students of queer studies, political sociology, social inequality, international relations, global studies, international justice, development studies, and the digital humanities.

Arnaud Kurze is an Associate Professor of Justice Studies at Montclair State University and a Global Fellow at the Wilson Center. He has published widely in academic journals, contributed to edited volumes and is the author of several reports on foreign affairs for government and international organizations. He is the co-author of *Justicecraft: Imagining Justice in Times of Conflict* (2024) and the book *Mapping Global Justice: Perspectives, Cases and Practices* (2023). He has been the recipient of many awards and fellowships, including Fulbright, the Library of Congress and the US State Department.

Sarah Sturken is a Research Associate at JusticeCraft Solutions, affiliated with McGill University, the University of Glasgow and Jagiellonian University. Her primary research interests lie in the history of the former Eastern Bloc, with a focus on memory politics, ethnonationalism, and illiberalism. Her work investigates the nexus of the politics of history and memory and nation-building in illiberal regimes. She is the recipient of multiple scholarships and awards, and has conducted research in Canada, the United States, Estonia, Poland, the United Kingdom, and Kazakhstan.

Steve Thwe is a Research Associate at JusticeCraft Solutions, holding a Master's degree in International Relations from New York University and former managing editor of the *Journal of Political Inquiry*. His primary research interests lie in the politics of South Asia, with a focus on conflict resolution, ethnonationalism, and democratic consolidation. His work explores the impact of governance systems on the emergence of violent or peaceful outcomes during periods of political contestation.

Routledge Research in Gender and Society

For more information about this series, please visit: https://www.routledge.com/
Routledge-Research-in-Gender-and-Society/book-series/SE0271

Mapping Queerness in Times of Uncertainty

Stories of Struggle, Invisibility and Space

Arnaud Kurze, Sarah Sturken and Steve Thwe

Routledge
Taylor & Francis Group

LONDON AND NEW YORK

First published 2025
by Routledge
4 Park Square, Milton Park, Abingdon, Oxon OX14 4RN

and by Routledge
605 Third Avenue, New York, NY 10158

Routledge is an imprint of the Taylor & Francis Group, an informa business

British Library Cataloguing-in-Publication Data
A catalogue record for this book is available from the British Library

ISBN: 978-1-032-93438-9 (hbk)
ISBN: 978-1-032-93439-6 (pbk)
ISBN: 978-1-003-56587-1 (ebk)

DOI: 10.4324/9781003565871

Typeset in Times New Roman
by KnowledgeWorks Global Ltd.

To the resilient spirits who traverse unseen paths and create spaces of hope amidst adversity.

To the activists, scholars, and communities whose unwavering courage and creativity inspire us daily.

And to everyone who believes in the power of visibility and the strength of solidarity in the face of oppression.

This book is for you.

Contents

Figures

Preface
Global Queer Spaces in a World in Flux

In the landscape of global LGBTQ advocacy, the past few decades have witnessed significant strides toward equality and visibility. However, these advancements are often met with new challenges, particularly in regions grappling with sociopolitical instability, cultural conservatism, and ecological crises. *Mapping Queerness in Times of Uncertainty: Stories of Struggle, Invisibility, and Space* seeks to navigate these complex terrains, offering a fresh perspective on the spaces—both literal and metaphorical—where queer communities strive for recognition and rights amidst adversity.

This book emerges from a collaboration between three distinct voices, each bringing a unique expertise to the table. Dr. Arnaud Kurze of Montclair State University (and a Global Fellow at the Wilson Center), Sarah Sturken of the University of Glasgow and Uniwersytet Jagielloński, and Steve Thwe of JusticeCraft Solutions, together weave a narrative that is as diverse as it is cohesive. Our collective goal is to chart the often unseen and unmapped territories of queer struggle, illustrating how LGBTQ communities adapt, resist, and flourish under varying conditions of oppression and marginalization.

We are conscious that queer communities are highly diverse and heterogeneous, which is further accentuated by the geographic, social, political and cultural conditions on the ground. Therefore, our selective case studies can serve as food for thought for similar contexts, serving as a catalyst for further scholarly inquiry to generate nuanced understandings of different global queer spaces.

As our title indicates, at the heart of our exploration is the concept of space—how it is contested, constructed, and experienced by queer individuals and groups. The notion of space extends beyond geographical boundaries to include digital realms, cultural landscapes, and the liminal zones of societal norms and expectations, drawing and building on conceptual notions by French sociologist Pierre Bourdieu and French historian and philosopher Michel Foucault. By employing digital mapping tools and critical cartography, we visualize these spaces in innovative ways, shedding light on the interactions and networks that sustain queer activism across different regions.

Our journey begins with a theoretical framework that integrates insights from queer studies, international relations, political sociology, and digital humanities. This interdisciplinary approach allows us to dissect the multifaceted nature of queer spaces in times of uncertainty, emphasizing the interplay between local and global dynamics, postcolonial legacies, and ever-evolving socio-political climates. Through a series of case studies spanning the Middle East, North Africa, Southeast Asia, Eastern Europe, and Russia, we delve into specific contexts that shape queer experiences and activism in these regions.

In the Middle East and North Africa (MENA) region, we explore how social media and collective action create fragile yet resilient spaces of deliberation for sexual minorities amidst political transitions. We then shift our focus to Tunisia and Lebanon, examining how art and activism intertwine to carve out spaces for LGBTQ communities in the face of democratic stagnation. In Singapore, we confront the legacy of neocolonialism and its impact on queer advocacy, while in Poland, we scrutinize the role of religion and illiberalism in shaping queer struggles. The Russian case study highlights the perilous environment for queer activism under autocratic regimes and the strategies employed to navigate such hostile terrains.

Our final chapter synthesizes these diverse narratives into an eclectic cartography of queer stakeholders and subversive activities, offering a meta-analysis that transcends individual case studies. The empirical findings complement the conceptual framework laid out at the outset of our book. Yet they do not constitute an attempt to fuel broad sweeping and widely generalizable insights. Rather they aim to inspire further research and activism, providing a critical lens through which scholars, practitioners, advocates, and students can engage with the ongoing challenges and triumphs of queer communities worldwide.

Mapping Queerness in Times of Uncertainty is not just a scholarly endeavor but a call to action. It underscores the importance of visibility, the power of space, and the resilience of those who continue to fight for their rights against formidable odds. We hope that this work will contribute to a deeper understanding of the intricate and often invisible struggles faced by LGBTQ individuals and communities, fostering a more inclusive and just world.

New York, United States
Kraków, Poland
New York, United States
July 2024

Arnaud Kurze
Sarah Sturken
Steve Thwe

Acknowledgments
Queer and Allied Support Throughout

This book's origins date back to one of the co-authors' fieldwork in the MENA region, particularly Tunisia and Lebanon in 2015 and 2016, spanning almost a decade of data, observations, and reflections that have helped forge and mold the current work completed with two other co-authors. This project couldn't have been done without the support of several academic, policy, and scholarly institutions, including the Issam Fares Institute for Public Policy and International Affairs, JusticeCraft Solutions, the Library of Congress' Kluge Center, Montclair State University, New York University, the Orient Institut Beirut, University of Sousse, University of Tunis, and the Wilson Center, among others.

The constructive and invaluable feedback from colleagues, peers, and friends at several professional conferences, including but not limited to the American Political Science Association, the International Studies Association, and the Law and Society Association, has been instrumental. Many professional associations have created platforms for greater visibility of lesbian, gay, bisexual, transgender, and queer (LGBTQ) and other gender and sexual minorities. Instead of operating in a conceptual and intellectual vacuum, these spaces are inherently intersectional and provide opportunities for transdisciplinary inquiries and transversal collaborations, inviting stakeholders to draw connections and explore intricate issues from a holistic perspective. We are grateful for the resources, networks, and opportunities created by these different communities.

Moreover, we are deeply indebted to those at the forefront of promoting LGBTQ activism and advocacy, striving for equal rights for gender and sexual minorities around the world. Their participation and willingness to share their stories made this book possible. While the road to achieving these goals is still long and rocky, important strides have been made, and continue to help forge a path forward.

The unwavering support of the editorial team at Routledge, led by Emily Briggs, brought this project to fruition. We are tremendously grateful to three anonymous reviewers who provided very helpful comments and suggestions to strengthen our work and ensure the book is a meaningful resource for all those interested in this topic. We would also like to thank the following individuals for their thoughtful comments and edits of earlier drafts of this book: Celia Burns, Michael Schroeder, and Sarah Singh.

Introduction
Setting the Stage for Queer Spaces

The landscape of Lesbian, Gay, Bisexual, Transgender, and Queer (LGBTQ) communities has evolved significantly in recent years, navigating through the complexities of social, political, and ecological uncertainties. The book at hand ventures into uncharted territories, offering a critical perspective on emerging and alternative spaces for emancipation within LGBTQ communities across various geographic regions. This exploration is particularly pertinent in a world where the rift between liberal, western values and more conservative cultural norms, especially in postcolonial countries, continues to deepen. This introduction sets the stage for understanding the nuanced struggles and innovative spaces different LGBTQ communities occupy and create amidst these challenges.

Queer studies have made remarkable strides in the past decade, not only raising awareness about gender and sexual minorities and identity politics but also transforming scholarly discourse in international studies and global justice. Scholars like Picq and Thiel have highlighted the significance of identity politics (Picq and Thiel 2015), while Weber and Mason have each underscored the impact of queer studies on international relations (Mason 2018; Weber 2016). Kurze and Lamont further elucidate the role of Queer Theory in global justice (2022). Amidst these advancements, the concept of space, both physical and metaphorical, has gained prominence, with scholars like Ramos and Mowlabocus or Puar, Rushbrook, and Schein each delving into its implications for LGBTQ communities (Puar, Rushbrook, and Schein 2003; Ramos and Mowlabocus 2020).

This book aims to push the boundaries further by providing a theoretical framework for lesser-studied spaces within this context and advancing digital mapping tools to visualize these trends. It pursues three principal objectives, centered around key themes. First, it introduces a conceptual framework that intersects international relations, global studies, political sociology, and digital humanities. This interdisciplinary approach leverages the authors' extensive field experience and theoretical insights to present an untold narrative from a novel and crucial perspective. Utilizing data visualization tools embedded in critical cartography studies, the book offers a holistic and nuanced picture of LGBTQ struggles across diverse contexts and time periods.

DOI: 10.4324/9781003565871-1

The breadth of case studies included in this work allows for a comprehensive understanding of the transitional experiences of vulnerable, often unheard actors and groups. These experiences are examined against the backdrop of sociopolitical variables such as democratization, religion, and postcolonial tensions. The book showcases the intricate and multilayered issues these communities face, underscoring the complexity and diversity of LGBTQ struggles globally, going beyond a universal human rights approach that was commonly seen in earlier discussions on such issues.

We recognize that queer communities are incredibly diverse and varied, shaped by the unique geographic, social, political, and cultural contexts they inhabit. As such, our carefully chosen case studies are intended to offer valuable insights applicable to similar situations and are not meant to create broad, sweeping generalizations. Instead, these case studies aim to spark further academic investigation, fostering a deeper and more nuanced understanding of the myriad queer experiences and spaces across the globe.

One of the distinguishing features of this book is its emphasis on the intricacies of contemporary spaces where sexual and gender minorities strive for visibility, voice, and rights. We are keenly aware of the limitations that exist when ascribing any generalized or universal queer experience across such varied localities, and instead aim to do justice to the unique environments where these issues are contested. The book's interdisciplinary theoretical perspective relies heavily on postmodern and sociological frameworks. Concepts of space, agency, and network approaches are central to this analysis. Unlike many handbooks or edited volumes, this work is a fully co-authored monograph, providing a cohesive and powerful narrative of ideas. Our reliance on digital visualization tools and mapping efforts further enhances the accessibility of the results, enabling scholars, practitioners, advocates, and students to grasp intricate cross-regional trends through cutting-edge digital technology.

The structure of the book is designed to guide the reader through the multifaceted issues and themes explored. Our intro sets the stage for the journey, providing an overview of the book's objectives and significance. The first part, "Mapping New Global Queer Spaces," includes two chapters that lay the theoretical groundwork and introduce digital visualization tools. Chapter 1 delves into the emerging and alternative spaces for emancipation within LGBTQ communities, highlighting the conceptual and methodological barriers to advancing knowledge in this field. Chapter 2 utilizes digital mapping tools to illustrate synergies among community members across different geographic areas, proposing a roadmap to further capture the evolution of cross-regional dynamics.

The second part, "Struggles in Contested Queer Spaces," comprises five chapters that offer in-depth case studies from various regions. Chapter 3 explores the creation of alternative spaces for sexual minorities during political transitions, focusing on the role of social media and collective action in the Middle East and North Africa. Chapter 4 examines how art serves as a medium to create innovative spaces of deliberation amidst political stagnation or regression specifically in Tunisia and Lebanon. Chapter 5 analyzes the non-confrontational modes of LGBTQ activism in a pragmatic and postcolonial context, homing in on Singapore. Chapter 6 investigates the development of queer activism in an illiberal context, examining the influence of student activism and the cultivation of refugee spaces in Poland. Chapter 7 focuses on the repressive politics in autocratic regimes and the resilience-driven underground mode of queer activism in Russia.

The final part, "A Queer Topography," culminates in Chapter 8, which offers a meta-analysis of the issues and provides a transversal view of different collective actions and contentious politics. This chapter provides an array of subversive activities in repressive sociopolitical and cultural contexts, complementing the conceptual framework outlined at the outset of our book to better understand the daily struggles of LGBTQ communities across various regions. Our conclusion ties together the themes explored in the book, reflecting on the broader implications of the research. The authors emphasize the interconnectedness of LGBTQ struggles with global socio-political and ecological changes, providing insights for further research and advocacy.

The book's interdisciplinary approach, innovative use of digital visualization tools, and comprehensive case studies make it a valuable resource for a wide range of readers. It offers groundbreaking insights for scholars, students, policymakers, and practitioners working on issues related to human rights, sexual and gender-based injustice, and queer studies. The holistic and nuanced narrative presented in this book contributes significantly to the growing scholarship in these fields, highlighting the intertwined nature of LGBTQ struggles with broader socio-political developments.

We address a crucial gap in existing literature by providing a comprehensive theoretical framework that bridges the divide between theory and practice. While previous works have offered valuable insights into specific aspects of Queer Theory and LGBTQ activism, this book's strength lies in its overarching theoretical grounding and interdisciplinary perspective. It provides readers with a conceptual toolkit to navigate the complex landscape of LGBTQ struggles and offers practical considerations for local stakeholders dealing with global issues.

In conclusion, our work represents a significant contribution to the field of queer studies and beyond. By mapping new global queer spaces, examining struggles in contested spaces, and offering a queer topography of subversive activities, it provides a comprehensive and critical perspective on the evolving landscape of LGBTQ communities. The innovative use of digital mapping tools and the interdisciplinary approach make it an essential resource for understanding and addressing the multifaceted challenges faced by LGBTQ communities in times of social, political, and ecological uncertainty. Next we will delve into the conceptual framework of this book, further exploring the notion of space in this context.

References

Kurze, Arnaud, and Christopher K. Lamont. 2022. *Mapping Global Justice: Perspectives, Cases and Practice*. Oxfordshire: Routledge.

Mason, Corinne L. 2018. *Routledge Handbook of Queer Development Studies*. Abingdon: Routledge.

Picq, M. L., and M. Thiel. 2015. *Sexualities in World Politics: How LGBTQ Claims Shape International Relations*. Interventions. Taylor & Francis.

Puar, Jasbir Kaur, Dereka Rushbrook, and Louisa Schein. 2003. "Sexuality and Space: Queering Geographies of Globalization." *Environment and Planning. D, Society & Space* 21 (4): 383–87.

Ramos, R., and S. Mowlabocus. 2020. "Queer Sites in Global Contexts: Technologies, Spaces, and Otherness." https://books.google.com/books?hl=en&lr=&id=w6oLEA AAQBAJ&oi=fnd&pg=PP1&dq=queer+space+global&ots=Vs_mKZXYlJ&sig=W 3MPjKwRI4lS1dUC0PNljMKmtsk

Weber, Cynthia. 2016. *Queer International Relations: Sovereignty, Sexuality and the Will to Knowledge*. Oxford: Oxford University Press.

Part 1
Mapping Global Queer Spaces

The part comprises two chapters establishing the theoretical foundation and introducing digital visualization tools. Chapter 1 explores the new and alternative spaces for Lesbian, Gay, Bisexual, Transgender, and Queer community emancipation, emphasizing the conceptual and methodological challenges in advancing this field. Chapter 2 employs digital mapping tools to demonstrate the synergies among community members across various regions, suggesting a framework to better understand the development of cross-regional dynamics.

DOI: 10.4324/9781003565871-2

1 Queer Theory and Space in Times of Uncertainty

Whether in Asia, with the *Sayan* network[1], or in Latin America, with the project *Adelante*[2], Lesbian, Gay, Bisexual, Transgender, and Queer (LGBTQ)[3] activism has seen larger participation and collaboration across different countries and regions. Some of these initiatives receive funding from Global North partners, such as the European Union (EU) for activities including workshops, advocacy, and campaigns to increase the visibility and acceptance of sexual minorities. Recent work by LGBTQ communities in non-Western-centric states has fueled collaborative practices unique to local contexts, challenging the "gay international" (Massad 2007)—a predominantly Western-driven LGBTQ discourse—and contributing to a nuanced landscape of synergies between various groups. This is a great starting point for revisiting ideas of Postcoloniality in queer studies, and reframing questions LGBTQ communities face in challenging times, notably with the rise of illiberalism and homophobia.

While this book uses the concept of LGBTQ communities to refer to broader struggles faced by sexual minorities, the authors are aware that communities are social constructs (Anderson 1991) with wide-ranging effects on the daily lives of their members. Identity plays a key role in group formation, particularly for members of sexual minority groups against the backdrop of changing contexts and conditions. Recent work has underscored the importance of accentuating nuances, challenges, and even tensions among members of a larger community across various topical issues (Edenborg 2020; Monro 2020; Hagai and Seymour 2022; Pain 2022). Our book aims to add to these cases, providing complementary empirical evidence based on several case studies included here.

Our understanding of uncertainty draws from the writings of Helga Nowotny, who states that "the tighter coupling of impact expectations with the higher degree of certainty that knowledge is expected to have in order to meet the target leads to new uncertainties" (Nowotny 2015, Chapter 1). In this context, increasing illiberal tendencies, impending ecological disasters, and regional conflicts have also affected the creation of queer spaces in less-developed LGBTQ communities. Relying on spatial theory is essential, as it

DOI: 10.4324/9781003565871-3

allows for a richer understanding of sexual minorities' varying engagements in diverse settings. The core of our book seeks to better understand LGBTQ voices during political change, yet our research concludes with forward-looking reflections on a growing field of scholarly inquiry at the intersection of climate change and its consequences for vulnerable populations, such as sexual minorities.

To better understand who is involved across and in what type of activities stakeholders engage, we scrutinize contemporary queer literature against the backdrop of postcolonial legacies. We then employ spatial theory (Bilić 2016; Hartal 2016; Mutua-Mambo 2020; Voiculescu and Groza 2021), showing that barriers to advancing our knowledge of queer studies are primarily conceptual and methodological. To underscore this growing phenomenon, we examine impediments to empowering local communities and networks beyond national boundaries, providing an initial cross-cutting visualization on a series of regional case studies.

Our work spans several continents including in-depth case studies of Lebanon, Tunisia, Singapore, Poland, and Russia, as well as references to other Asian, African, and Americas examples. We are aware that we cannot provide a systematic and comprehensive cross-regional analysis of various issues. Instead, our carefully selected cases are characterized by specific institutional and systemic features to provide valuable comparative data, allowing for a nuanced analysis and better understanding of recent trends within specific queer communities. Our ultimate goal is to provide new and layered insights about the contemporary struggles and consequences of queer activities and engagement in different contexts.

The ethical considerations for this research are paramount, given its focus on vulnerable LGBTQ communities in diverse geopolitical contexts. We adhered to robust ethical principles when carrying out our research, prioritizing the anonymity and confidentiality of participants to mitigate risks of harm. This necessitated stringent anonymization protocols and explicit informed consent from all participants. Our research's postcolonial grounding demands a critical examination of power dynamics between researchers and participants. We adopted a participatory approach, involving community members in the research process to foster trust and ensure the research benefits the communities involved. Employing local ethical guidelines and collaborating with local researchers helps mitigate power imbalances and ensures culturally sensitive research practices. When employing digital visualization tools, we approached them with caution to ensure they do not inadvertently reveal sensitive information.

Queer Theory, Emerging Voices, and Space

Global and transnational LGBTQ issues have garnered attention for some time, including advocacy-driven analysis and academic inquiries from various disciplines (Kollman and Waites 2009; Moreau 2017; Roth 2015;

Wieringa and Sívori 2013). Against the backdrop of contemporary queer literature and postcolonial legacies, we examine countries with emerging queer voices to capture varying factors, such as socioeconomic priorities, cultural and religious influences, and political conditions. This section highlights the importance of scrutinizing developments within sexual minority communities by borrowing from space-oriented studies.

Striving to Contextualize the (In)Visible

Queer studies have made strides in recent years to disclose areas that have long been overlooked. While many of these areas are expanding, they need continued dedicated research that often requires engaging directly with the LGBTQ community. Queer issues are oftentimes not prioritized due to seemingly larger importance of more visible issues such as food scarcity and political stability. One issue relates to the "medicalisation of sexualities" as a consequence of colonial practices, particularly in the Global South (Chappell 2019, 7). Transnational LGBTQ activism has flourished and issues pertaining directly to queer migration and questions of state protection and safe spaces for sexual minorities are developing across case studies and regions (Valiquette, Cowper-Smith, and Su 2021). We will develop the question of citizenship below.

Questions surrounding the power of language and discourse, notably in promoting queer thinking, have gained increased scholarly traction recently (Singh 2021). The role of academic discourse and literary forms of expression addressing LGBTQ issues has become more visible. In other spheres, conservative forces have also harnessed discourse power to push evangelical Christian narratives, such as in South Korea (Yi, Jung, and Phillips 2017) and in Singapore (see Chapter 5). Our book addresses conservative voices in two cases: in Singapore, instrumentalizing an East–West dichotomy and in Central and Eastern Europe, using Poland as an example where conservatives pitch the Europeanization discourse as a threat to Polish norm. In Russia, we examine the effects of repressive politics in autocratic regimes, using the war in Ukraine as a context. The significance of online spaces for LGBTQ communities, including their empowering potential, has been at the forefront of scholarly inquiry (Yue and Lim 2022). Online ethnographies and AI as tools to promote less visible communities are trends captured here.

Increased visibility of LGBTQ research in less explored areas has taken on various forms in recent years, including scholarship promotion via non-mainstream avenues, linking advocacy and psychological trends and LGBTQ discourse, and fueling an action research agenda and community alliance formation in different regions from Latin America all the way to Southeast Asia (Cornejo Salinas, Martínez, and Vidal-Ortiz 2020; Manalastas and Torre 2016; Nicol, Gates-Gasse, and Mule 2014; Tellis and Bala 2016). To increase visibility our book employs data visualization tools relying on mapping software, including ArcGIS. Mapping, as construed within the parameters of our research objectives, does not only include attempts at capturing diverse engagements by different queer communities across separate geographic regions. It also encompasses a critical, spatially oriented analysis of practices, challenges, and conditions on the ground within specific queer communities, which we further elaborate on in this chapter's section on geographies of sexualities. While Chapter 2 introduces our readers to the methodological nuts and bolts of geo-mapping and data visualization with cartographic data from a global perspective, Chapter 8 offers more granular narratives and map-based renderings to provide readers with a rich meta-analysis that builds upon our findings and research outputs.

Furthermore, scrutinizing LGBTQ issues against the backdrop of postcolonial legacies and power imbalances, some recent work has emphasized the importance of "strategic universalism" (Lara 2018). First coined by Paul Gilroy (2000) with respect to race, in the context of Dominican LGBTQ activism, the concept demonstrates the grassroots power of minority organizing and community-building to oppose the grip of the Catholic Church, the corrupt state, and anti-LGBTQ values. "It also reveals how the struggles of Dominican LGBT subjects takes place through global governance and in response to global Catholic fundamentalist authorities" (Lara 2018, 112). The Dominican case illustrates the importance of intersectional issues that pertain not only to gender or race but also include health and socioeconomic factors (Aylward 2019).

Economic disparities are closely linked to broader development questions associated with development issues. As Julie Moreau and Ashley Currier have pointed out, development assistance programs from the Global North pose a "queer dilemma" especially for African LGBTQ activists. The latter cannot refuse funding from organizations, yet the ties expose the vulnerabilities of LGBTQ advocates groups "to both heteronormative and homonormative pressures that buttress neocolonial power relations" (Moreau and Currier 2018, 223). Reminiscent to the work mentioned on disabilities above, research that links development studies and Queer Theory is crucial to further illuminate power imbalances and struggles in these contexts. The questioning of the current North-centric development discourse has led to increased awareness of heteronormative practices, including NGOs such as the *Human Dignity Trust* (Francesca Stella et al. 2015). It also sparked discussions on how to best integrate religion into the equation, especially when transnational religious networks can create tension within local politics, such as Evangelical conservatism in Singapore.

Development issues are also closely linked to questions of identity politics and citizenship at the nation-state level. In terms of queer identities in non-Western contexts, this becomes visible Euro- or US-centric sexual citizenship. Homonationalism, as some argue, has led to further undermining the heterogeneity in sexual identities and queerness. This poses a particular problem in terms of societies in former colonies, as it reintroduces orientalist practices and a colonized otherness, creating linkages that are easily exploited by conservative voices in painting queer inclusivity as a foreign import (Sabsay 2012; see also Stella, Taylor, and Reynolds 2015). These trends further exacerbate the dichotomy between Western-centric practices and peripheral states' narratives toward their societies. As a result, "sexual democracy has become an instrument for governments to implement other discriminations based on cultural, religious or racial differences" (Sabsay 2012, 613).

Democratizing practices, however, do not necessarily lead to negative consequences. On the contrary, increasing the rule of law may have a positive effect on society where politics and law intersect. Jurisprudential gains have been made in Latin America over the past decade and advocacy educational campaigns in Chile, for instance, have led to broader LGBTQ acceptance and even promotion of LGBTQ rights (Miles and Zelada 2021). Given the postcolonial struggle of many nations across the Global South, for some, legal gains are embedded in transformative constitutions that rose after the suffering of the oppressed, such as in South Africa. The South African constitution, as a case in point, "expressly recognized sexual orientation as a prohibited basis of discrimination in the new South African state" (Narrain 2014). And in India, long known for legal practices based on a colonial penal code of 1860 criminalizing sodomy, the Supreme Court decriminilaized consensual same-se or sexual conduct in a 2018 ruling (BBC News 2018). The above examples raise the question of cultural factors fueling transformative change at an institutional and structural level, which we address next.

Postcolonial Legacies

Closely examining the social transformation of societies in view of promoting LGBTQ rights proves helpful to further understand collaborative trends and exchanges of LGBTQ communities across the Global South. While Latin America has witnessed LGBTQ rights advances over the last few decades—underlined by a wave of judicial assertiveness—high-profile cases of personalities that are out, especially in politics, remain rare (Corrales 2015). In addition, the region is also witnessing a backlash with religious groups, particularly the evangelical church, drawing on liberal democratic institutions to hamper progress made by LGBTQ advocates (Corrales 2020).

Yet growing awareness of power imbalances rooted in postcolonial legacies has resulted in strategies and research to support LGBTQ communities through alternative funding opportunities connecting local NGOs in the Global South with donors around the world (Becker et al. 2018). An online portal, *Funders for LGBTQ Issues*, a US-based network, demonstrates the challenges when grappling with funding. It stated in its 2017–2018 report that only 31% of the donations went to countries of the Global South with the majority of the money being distributed to countries in the Global

North.[4] Other cases illustrate that LGBTQ funding now goes beyond the initial HIV donor support, such as in Southeast Asia, but grants also remain modest in Malaysia and Singapore (Ng 2018). The latter is an excellent illustration of how the rights of the LGBTQ community "ebb and flow with the political and economic conditions of the nation" where homosexuality is still criminalized (Ciocchini and Radics 2019). Economic security is valued more than political freedom.

The dark shadow of lingering colonial practices remains visible in countries of the North notably when scrutinizing asylum cases of LGBTQ refugees. For example, "interconnected structures of colonial discourse and regulation come into force through the Canadian asylum and resettlement process" (Fobear 2014). Here, it is important to ask not only the question of where asylum seekers come from but also where they are going. In other words, Canada's silence on and the neglect of Indigenous issues especially in terms of migration studies is telling in this context (Fobear 2014). It is thus important to create greater visibility for those who have been marginalized. This also holds true for specific minority groups of the LGBTQ community, such as trans and gender-diverse (see, for instance, Essack, Van Pol, and Ndelu 2018). Growing levels of consciousness in this regard have driven Northern donor countries to questionable awareness-raising practices, showcasing LGBTQ advances in the Global South in a Northern context.[5]

The illustrations trigger two essential observations. On the one hand, LGBTQ activists worldwide despite uncountable struggles and challenges have fueled a global mobilization of LGBTQ rights and created a connection between a broader set of civil and individual rights and a human rights agenda (R. Thoreson 2020). While synergies emerged between the North and South, countless tensions rose along the way. For advocacy to be successful, it was also necessary to explore different avenues, such as an educational route in Chile or Argentina, when non-binary students were ejected from school (R. R. Thoreson 2014, 186). Moreover, it required creative searches for suitable coalition partners, some more evident and reliable than others, including advocates of the Convention of the Elimination of All Forms of Discrimination Against Women (CEDAW) (R. R. Thoreson 2014, 1). On the other hand, the universality discourse about human rights has also proven to be counterproductive in different cultural or regional contexts, especially when promoting LGBTQ rights. Brokers, therefore, must walk a fine line between specificity and universal claims (R. R. Thoreson 2014, 212).

As a result, being sensitive to the effects of power differentials, institutional, and structural impediments, as well as diverse contexts and backgrounds of stakeholders engaged in these processes, is a fundamental premise for understanding shifting trends across the Global South and beyond. The notion of space is especially useful to draw from here, which we explore below.

Geographies of Sexualities and In-between Spaces

Addressing LGBTQ issues from a spatial lens is not new. In fact, critical theory has incorporated geographies of sexualities as a burgeoning scholarly effort to explore the linkages between geographical and regional factors in view of different sexual minorities' challenges across varying case studies(Browne, Brown, and Nash 2021; Datta et al. 2020; Kazyak 2020; March 2021; Shirinian 2021; Zhou, Sinding, and Goellnicht 2021). This book draws from this rich canon of work to further explore spatial-oriented frameworks to help better understand the queer landscapes in socially and politically changing contexts. As a case in point, Andrew Tucker addresses important questions related to international engagement in view of LGBTQ issues in the Global South, notably pointing to the "sometimes-problematic deployment of discourses that emerged initially in the Global North onto places such as sub-Saharan Africa" (Tucker 2020, 684). He engages with discourse practices and perceptions as well as the legitimacy of human rights, notably from a health perspective. In our work, we seek to further our understanding of *how* spaces are used and occupied by different queer stakeholders across different contexts. Conceptually we largely draw on French sociologist Pierre Bourdieu and his field theory as well as notions of *habitus* and "capital" (see, for instance, Bourdieu 1993). In sociology, field theory explores how individuals and groups construct their social environment (or fields), and how they are affected by such fields. While his work has been applied to diverse disciplines and contexts, including international relations theory (see, for instance, Bigo 2011), our interest lies particularly with the peripheral, liminal spaces, or so-called "inbetween spaces" (Kurze and Lamont 2021). As some have pointed out, relying on the latter allows one to better "understand the dynamics of new emerging voices" within specific queer groups and their impact beyond their immediate communities (Kurze and Lamont 2021, 157). It also enables us to explore challenges experienced by members of different queer communities in different contexts.

As seen earlier, the notion of space does not only refer to physical and tangible spaces but also virtual ones, such as the internet. Interactions between these two spheres are common, such as an organization or social movement's presence on a social media platform like Facebook or Instagram and its engagement with the community, including events, educational programs, or protest marches. Urban spaces in national contexts with a hostile LGBTQ environment are an example of an intertwined web of spaces and actors. LGBTQ advocacy, if illegal, often requires strategic alliances with supportive partners, such as women's organizations (Tucker and Hassan 2020). As a consequence, international organizations, such as the United Nations, have taken note of the importance of gender in urban planning strategies with regard to sustainable development goals. The combination of promoting gender inclusiveness in urban spaces proves therefore also beneficial for LGBTQ communities to form and grow networks for advocacy purposes (Chant and McIlwaine 2015, 48). Yet, as some have noted, the appropriation of space, notably in urban areas, such as major cities, is not a linear process and comes with territorial challenges, including contestations by heteronormative forces when LGBTQ communities find themselves in conservative and hostile enclaves, geographically and socially speaking (Costa and Amorim 2019, 4). So-called "LGBT free zones" are indicative of this trend (Dunin-Wąsowicz 2023).

This phenomenon is further compounded by the notion of "gay menace" put forward by many repressive states to ostracize sexual minority groups. Forms of state homophobia are problematic insofar as they decontextualize sexual minority politics, thus limiting a rights-based discourse to achieve security for sexual and gender minorities under threat (Bosia 2020). Closely linked to this is the issue of sexual citizenship or the question of space with regard to sexualities and citizens, which requires a certain level of privacy. Autocratic regimes, however, often deprived citizens of these private spaces, aiming for societal conformity and homogeneity. More so, autocratic non-Western states often frame queerness as a Western import, illustrating the intersection of postcolonialism and repression. In addition, social, economic, and other realities affect the practice of such citizenship forms, further marginalizing LGBTQ communities (Richardson 2017). The poisonous relationship between sexuality and citizenship in illiberal states further plays out in the politics of space and the promotion of the nation-state. As an example, LGBTQ mainstreaming against the backdrop of homonationalism and homonormativity although inclusive at first sight, creates exclusionary effects — especially for LGBTQ subgroups—and has been appropriated by state authorities for other ends, such as in Israel, the "gay heaven" of the Middle East (Hartal and Sasson-Levy 2017, 741).

Despite state-centric challenges and repressive practices, LGBTQ stakeholders have continued to engage in grassroots transnational queer engagement and solidarity. A powerful illustration thereof is the "Queer University Video Capacity Building Training Program," a three-year initiative between Chinese and African queer filmmakers and activists in recent years, offering a participatory video production program (Bao 2020). Held mainly in Zimbabwe and Ghana, it highlights the importance of LGBTQ issues in development practices against the backdrop of the Chinese government's ambition on the African continent. Furthermore, it underscores the underlying potential harnessed by civil society to create a space and push the boundaries of the (in)visibility of sexual minorities through art.

As indicated above, digital technologies have played an important role in generating greater visibility for LGBTQ activism, particularly in sociopolitical contexts that are repressive and in which autocratic regimes target sexual minorities and marginalized groups. It must be noted, however, that under precarious conditions and at the risk of harassment, persecution, imprisonment, and violence, increased visibility might also require greater discretion and/or protective measures to ensure the safety of LGBTQ community members. Egypt, Tunisia, and Turkey all illustrate this phenomenon, when activists developed strategies to resist repression and to exist drawing from different social movement repertoires (Acconcia, Perego, and Perini 2022). As an example, Turkish students were able to connect across campuses, through networks and associations, including *Legato* and *Pembe Hayat* (Acconcia, Perego, and Perini 2022, 9). The use of social media under these attenuating circumstances is also crucial for some communities as it allows for the creation of alternative spaces to foster a collective identity in otherwise conservative surroundings (Mokhtar and Sukeri 2019).

The existence of safe spaces, physical and virtual, is vital to LGBTQ communities and has created opportunities for members to explore various forms of encounters, exchanges, and shared experiences. The fluid nature of these spaces, also referred to as Foucauldian *heterotopias* or spaces of otherness (Kurze 2020) serves as an excellent framework for this study to further explore the engagements and synergies between various stakeholders. We explore conceptual and empirical ramifications in this context in Chapters 3 and 4. As interactions between members of different LGBTQ communities vary it is crucial to also have a closer look at *where* exactly they connect, for *what* purpose, and *who* is getting together. The example of Turkish LGBTQ students organizing on, across, and beyond their campuses showcases how stakeholders operate in hybrid spaces or as mentioned above, in-between spaces. Getting to the bottom of these (in)visible sites and loci and framing an initial topographical map against the backdrop of the above conceptual foundations is next, starting with some methodological reflections. Drawing on Bourdieusian and Foucauldian notions when examining cases in our empirical excursion therefore provides conceptual grounding to better understand the daily struggles and challenges faced by various members of different queer communities in our selected cases.

Conclusion

This chapter introduced a critical perspective on alternative spaces for emancipation within LGBTQ communities across various regions in volatile times marked by increasing illiberal tendencies, ecological disasters, and regional conflicts. The term critical applies here in two ways. First, from a theoretical perspective by introducing spatial studies to LGBTQ issues within the context of heightened uncertainty and times of change. Second, in terms of applied mixed methods to process empirical data on the issue, which we will introduce in our next chapter. In fact, the digital visualization of synergies and collaborative efforts among different stakeholders using a digital mapping software tool, ArcGIS, constitutes an initial effort to visually and tangibly illustrate alliances and transnational and cross-regional work of LGBTQ advocacy groups and LGBTQ allies. Moreover, against the backdrop of recent

Queer Theory literature and postcolonial legacies, we used spatial concepts, particularly the idea of in-between spaces and introduced the notion of *heterotopias* (or spaces of otherness, which we further discuss in Chapter 3), to highlight the varying trends of LGBTQ stakeholders in different contexts and areas to promote justice and create greater visibility for marginalized and oppressed communities. Empowering local communities, however, is associated with intricate challenges and the exploratory maps provide an excellent opportunity to showcase some of these activities in a concise way.

Notes

1 See their official Facebook page at https://www.facebook.com/South-Asian-Young-queer-Activist-Network-338061486849872/about, accessed 1 September 2022.
2 See official project website at https://adelanteconladiversidad.com/, accessed 1 September 2022.
3 While different acronyms are used in the study of sexual minorities to capture the panoply of sexual and gender identities, the authors chose the commonly used acronym LGBTQ and may use the term "queer" as a term of reference despite the equivocal usage of the latter in the scholarly literature, see for instance (Worthen 2023)
4 See https://lgbtfunders.org/research-item/2017-2018-global-resources-report/, accessed 1 July 2024.
5 See https://humanityinaction.org/denmark-activities/gender-identity-in-the-global-south/, accessed 1 July 2024.

References

Acconcia, Giuseppe, Aurora Perego, and Lorenza Perini. 2022. "LGBTQ Activism in Repressive Contexts: The Struggle for (in)visibility in Egypt, Tunisia and Turkey." *Social Movement Studies,* 23(2), 2070225.

Anderson, Benedict. 1991. *Imagined Communities: Reflections on the Origin and Spread of Nationalism.* London: Verso.

Aylward, Erin. 2019. "Intergovernmental Organizations and Nongovernmental Organizations: The Development of an International Approach to LGBT Issues," January. https://doi.org/10.1093/oxfordhb/9780190673741.013.10.

Bao, Hongwei. 2020. "The Queer Global South: Transnational Video Activism between China and Africa." *Global Media and China* 5 (3): 294–318.

BBC News. 2018. "India Court Legalises Gay Sex in Landmark Ruling." *BBC*, September 6, 2018. https://www.bbc.com/news/world-asia-india-45429664.

Becker, Katrina, Hannah Bohn, Cody Raasch, and Richa Sharma. 2018. "LGBT Impact Travel Models for Connecting Potential Donors to LGBT Communities in the Global South." https://conservancy.umn.edu/handle/11299/208306.

Bigo, Didier. 2011. "Pierre Bourdieu and International Relations: Power of Practices, Practices of Power." *International Political Sociology* 5 (3): 225–58.

Bilić, Bojan. 2016. *LGBT Activism and Europeanisation in the Post-Yugoslav Space.* New York: Palgrave Macmillan.

Bosia, Michael J. 2020. "Global Sexual Diversity Politics and the Trouble with LGBT Rights." *In The Oxford Handbook of Global LGBT and Sexual Diversity Politics,* edited by Michael J. Bosia, Sandra M. McEvoy, and Momin Rahman, 433–449. Oxford: Oxford University Press.

Bourdieu, Pierre. 1993. *The Field of Cultural Production: Essays on Art and Literature.* Edited by Randal Johnson. 1st ed. New York: Columbia University Press.

Browne, K., G. Brown, and C. J. Nash. 2021. "Geography and Sexuality II: Homonormativity and Heteroactivism." *Human Geography.* https://journals.sagepub.com/doi/abs/10.1177/03091325211016087.

Chant, Sylvia, and Cathy McIlwaine. 2015. *Cities, Slums and Gender in the Global South: Towards a Feminised Urban Future.* Abingdon: Routledge.

Chappell, Paul. 2019. "Situating Disabled Sexual Voices in the Global South." In *Diverse Voices of Disabled Sexualities in the Global South*, edited by Paul Chappell and Marlene de Beer, 1–25. Cham: Springer International Publishing.

Ciocchini, Pablo, and George Radics. 2019. *Criminal Legalities in the Global South: Cultural Dynamics, Political Tensions, and Institutional Practices.* Cham: Routledge.

Cornejo Salinas, Giancarlo, Juliana Martínez, and Salvador Vidal-Ortiz. 2020. "LGBT Studies Without LGBT Studies: Mapping Alternative Pathways in Perú and Colombia." *Journal of Homosexuality* 67 (3): 417–34.

Corrales, Javier 2015. "LGBT Rights and Representation in Latin America and the Caribbean: The Influence of Structure, Movements, Institutions, and Culture." LGBT Representation and Rights Initiative University of North Carolina at Chapel Hill. https://victoryinstitute.org/wp-content/uploads/2017/05/LAC-LGBT-PoliticalRepresentation-Report.pdf. Chapel Hill.

Corrales, Javier. 2020. "The Expansion of LGBT Rights in Latin America and the Backlash." In *The Oxford Handbook of Global LGBT and Sexual Diversity Politics*, edited by Michael J. Bosia, Sandra M. McEvoy, and Momin Rahman, 185–200. Oxford University Press.

Costa, Pedro, and Simone Amorim. 2019. "Queering the City. Spatiality and Territoriality of LGBT Lives in the Cities of Southern Europe and the Global South." *Cidades. Comunidades E Territórios*, 39. https://journals.openedition.org/cidades/1335.

Datta, A., P. Hopkins, L. Johnston, E. Olson, and J. M. Silva. 2020. *Routledge Handbook of Gender and Feminist Geographies.* https://api.taylorfrancis.com/content/books/mono/download?identifierName=doi&identifierValue=10.4324/9781315164748&type=googlepdf.

Dunin-Wąsowicz, Roch. 2023. "In Poland, the Home of 'LGBT-Free Zones', There Is Hope at Last for the Queer Community." *The Guardian*, November 1, 2023. https://www.theguardian.com/commentisfree/2023/nov/01/poland-lgbtq-new-government-law-and-justice-equality.

Edenborg, E. 2020. "Visibility in Global Queer Politics." In *The Oxford Handbook of Global LGBT and Sexual.* https://books.google.com/books?hl=en&lr=&id=9NfODwAAQBAJ&oi=fnd&pg=PA349&dq=queer+space+global&ots=OTiE-c0jRR&sig=PS-eYLYf39Bq0vBhbQSNP8VypH8.

Essack, Zaynab, Natasha Van der Pol, Sandile Ndelu, Joshua Sehoole, L.Leigh Ann Van der Meerwe, and Heidi Van Rooyen. 2018. "Putting the T in LGBT: Trans and Gender-Diverse (in) Visibility and Activism in South Africa." In *Civil Society in the Global South*, 149–57. https://doi.org/10.4324/9781315113579-9/putting-lgbt-zaynab-essack-natasha-van-der-pol-sandile-ndelu-joshua-sehoole-leigh-ann-van-der-merwe-heidi-van-rooyen.

Fobear, Katherine. 2014. "Queer Settlers: Questioning Settler Colonialism in LGBT Asylum Processes in Canada." *Refugee Reports* 30 (1): 47–56.

Gilroy, Paul. 2000. *Against Race: Imagining Political Culture Beyond the Color Line.* Cambridge: Harvard University Press.

Hagai, Ella Ben, and Nicole Seymour. 2022. "Is Lesbian Identity Obsolete?" *Journal of Lesbian Studies* 26 (1): 1–11.

Hartal, Gilly. 2016. "The Politics of Holding: Home and LGBT Visibility in Contested Jerusalem." *Gender, Place and Culture: A Journal of Feminist Geography* 23 (8): 1193–206.

Hartal, Gilly, and Orna Sasson-Levy. 2017. "Being [in] the Center: Sexual Citizenship and Homonationalism at Tel Aviv's Gay-Center." *Sexualities* 20 (5–6): 738–61.

Kazyak, Emily. 2020. "Introduction to Special Issue 'Geographies of Sexualities'." *Journal of Lesbian Studies* 24 (3): 173–85.

Kollman, Kelly, and Matthew Waites. 2009. "The Global Politics of Lesbian, Gay, Bisexual and Transgender Human Rights: An Introduction." *Contemporary Politics* 15 (1): 1–17.

Kurze, Arnaud. 2020. "Seeking New Metaphors: Gender Identities in Tunisia and Lebanon." In *Arab Spring: Modernity, Identity and Change*, edited by Eid Mohamed and Dalia Fahmy, 207–33. Cham: Springer International Publishing.

Kurze, Arnaud, and Christopher K. Lamont. 2021. "Breaking the Transitional Justice Machine: Exploring Spatiality, Space Travel, and Inbetween Spaces in Research Practice." *Political Anthropological Research on International Social Sciences (PARISS)* 2 (1): 155–78.

Lara, Ana-Maurine. 2018. "Strategic Universalisms and Dominican LGBT Activist Struggles for Civil and Human Rights." *Small Axe A Caribbean Journal of Criticism* 22 (2): 99–114.

Manalastas, Eric Julian, and Beatriz A. Torre. 2016. "LGBT Psychology in the Philippines." *Psychology of Sexualities Review* 7 (1): 60–72.

March, Loren. 2021. "Queer and Trans* Geographies of Liminality: A Literature Review." *Progress in Human Geography* 45 (3): 455–71.

Massad, Joseph. 2007. *Desiring Arabs.* Chicago, IL: University of Chicago Press.

Miles, Penny, and Carlos J. Zelada. 2021. "Introduction to: LGBTQIA + Rights Claiming in Latin America: Some Lessons from the Global South." *Bulletin of Latin American Research* 40 (5): 631–33.

Mokhtar, and Sukeri. 2019. "Social Media Roles in Spreading LGBT Movements in Malaysia." *Asian Journal of Media and Communication.* https://journal.uii.ac.id/AJMC/article/view/14310.

Monro, Surya. 2020. "Sexual and Gender Diversities: Implications for LGBTQ Studies." *Journal of Homosexuality* 67 (3): 315–24.

Moreau. 2017. "Political Science and the Study of LGBT Social Movements in the Global South." In *LGBTQ Politics: A Critical Reader.* edited by Marla Brettschneider, Susan Burgess, and Christine Keating, 439–57. New York: NYU Press. https://doi.org/10.18574/nyu/9781479849468.003.0031

Moreau, and Currier. 2018. "Queer Dilemmas: LGBT Activism and International Funding." *Routledge Handbook of Queer Development.* https://doi.org/10.4324/9781315529530-15/queer-dilemmas-julie-moreau-ashley-currier

Mutua-Mambo, C. Nthemba. 2020. "Living in a Liminal Space: Feminist and LGBT Alliances in Kenya." *Women's Studies in Communication* 43 (2): 125–30.

Narrain, Arvind. 2014. "Brazil, India, South Africa: Transformative Constitutions and Their Role in LGBT Struggles." *Sur - International Journal on Human Rights* 20:151.

Ng, Eve. 2018. "LGBT Advocacy and Transnational Funding in Singapore and Malaysia." *Development and Change* 49 (4): 1093–1114.

Nicol, Nancy, Erika Gates-Gasse, and Nick Mule. 2014. "Envisioning Global LGBT Human Rights: Strategic Alliances to Advance Knowledge and Social Change." *Scholarly and Research Communication* 5 (3). https://doi.org/10.22230/src.2014v5n3a165

Nowotny, H. 2015. "The Cunning of Uncertainty." https://books.google.com/books?h l=en&lr=&id=gGBcCwAAQBAJ&oi=fnd&pg=PT5&dq=The+Cunning+of+Uncert ainty&ots=Uc2kHl5xcR&sig=LGaTxB5X5PyhtsFubnUB8OkQhdU

Pain, Paromita. 2022. *LGBTQ Digital Cultures: A Global Perspective*. Abingdon: Routledge.

Richardson, Diane. 2017. "Rethinking Sexual Citizenship." *Sociology* 51 (2): 208–24.

Roth, Kenneth. 2015. "LGBT: Moving towards Equality." *Online Article. January* 23:P1.

Sabsay, Leticia. 2012. "The Emergence of the Other Sexual Citizen: Orientalism and the Modernisation of Sexuality." *Citizenship Studies* 16 (5–6): 605–23.

Shirinian, Tamar. 2021. "The Illiberal East: The Gender and Sexuality of the Imagined Geography of Eurasia in Armenia." *Gender, Place and Culture: A Journal of Feminist Geography* 28 (7): 955–74.

Singh, Jaspal Naveel. 2021. "Language, Gender and Sexuality in 2020: Forward Global South." *Gender & Language* 15 (2): 207–30. https://www.researchgate.net/ profile/Jaspal-Singh-19/publication/353402883_Language_gender_and_ sexuality_in_2020_forward_Global_South/links/60fa81861e95fe241a81281b/ Language-gender-and-sexuality-in-2020-forward-Global-South.pdf

Stella, F., Y. Taylor, and T. Reynolds. 2015. *Sexuality, Citizenship and Belonging: Trans-National and Intersectional Perspectives*. Edited by Francesca Stella, Yvette Taylor, Tracey Reynolds, and Antoine Rogers. Routledge Advances in Critical Diversities. Routledge. https://doi.org/10.4324/9781315752563.

Stella, Francesca, Yvette Taylor, Tracey Reynolds, and Antoine Rogers. 2015. "The New Trans-National Politics of LGBT Human Rights in the Commonwealth: What Can UK NGOs Learn from the Global South?" In *Sexuality, Citizenship and Belonging: Trans-National and Intersectional Perspectives*, edited by Francesca Stella, Yvette Taylor, Tracey Reynolds, and Antoine Rogers, 73–94. Routledge Advances in Critical Diversities. London: Routledge.

Tellis, Ashley, and Sruti Bala. 2016. *The Global Trajectories of Queerness: Re-Thinking Same-Sex Politics in the Global South*. Leiden: BRILL.

Thoreson, Ryan. 2020. "An International LGBT Movement." In *Oxford Research Encyclopedia of Politics*. Oxford: Oxford University Press.

Thoreson, Ryan R. 2014. *Transnational LGBT Activism: Working for Sexual Rights Worldwide*. Minneapolis: University of Minnesota Press.

Tucker, Andrew. 2020. "Geographies of Sexualities in Sub-Saharan Africa: Positioning and Critically Engaging with International Human Rights and Related Ascendant Discourses." *Progress in Human Geography* 44 (4): 683–703.

Tucker, Andrew, and Neil R. Hassan. 2020. "Situating Sexuality: An Interconnecting Research Agenda in the Urban Global South." *Geoforum; Journal of Physical, Human, and Regional Geosciences* 117 (December): 287–90.

Valiquette, Cowper-Smith, and Su. 2021. "Casa Miga: A Case of LGBT-Led, Transnational Activism in Latin America." *Sexualities*. https://doi.org/10.4324/9780429352102-13/casa-miga-tyler-valiquette-yuriko-cowper-smith-yvonne-su.

Voiculescu, Sorina, and Octavian Groza. 2021. "Legislating Political Space for LGBT Families: The 2018 Referendum on the Definition of Family in Romania." *Area* 53 (4): 679–90.

Wieringa, Saskia, and Horacio Sívori. 2013. The Sexual History of the Global South: Sexual Politics in Africa, *Asia and Latin America*. Bloomsbury: Bloomsbury Publishing.

Worthen, Meredith G. F. 2023. "Queer Identities in the 21st Century: Reclamation and Stigma." *Current Opinion in Psychology* 49 (February):101512.

Yi, Joseph, Gowoon Jung, and Joe Phillips. 2017. "Evangelical Christian Discourse in South Korea on the LGBT: The Politics of Cross-Border Learning." *Society* 54 (1): 29–33.

Yue, Audrey, and Ryan P. A. Lim. 2022. "Digital Sexual Citizenship and LGBT Young People's Platform Use." *International Communication Gazette* 84 (4): 331–48.

Zhou, Yanqiu Rachel, Christina Sinding, and Donald Goellnicht. 2021. *Sexualities, Transnationalism, and Globalisation: New Perspectives*. Abingdon: Routledge.

2   Visualizing (In)Visible Queer Communities

In the context of growing sociopolitical and ecological uncertainties, mentioned in our previous chapter, understanding the evolving landscape of different LGBTQ communities within a global context is crucial. This chapter emphasizes empowering local communities and networks beyond national boundaries through exploratory visualizations of regional case studies. It builds on our theoretical groundwork by presenting an exploratory dataset compiled from diverse online sources. Sensitive data has been removed to protect local stakeholders. Employing a mixed-method approach, this chapter integrates qualitative analysis with digital visualization, utilizing digital mapping tools to highlight interactions among LGBTQ stakeholders across different regions and time periods. It discusses the challenges inherent in cartographic research and lays the groundwork for additional, more detailed visualized mapping data presented in Chapter 8. By capturing cross-regional dynamics and the emancipatory power of online communities, the chapter aims to illustrate the synergies and obstacles these different communities face, providing a comprehensive understanding of their evolving practices and trends.

Mapping Global Inbetween Spaces of Different LGBTQ Communities[1]

In our previous chapter, we explored the concept of inbetween spaces, underlining justice-driven challenges in repressive contexts. We now focus on initial efforts to capture and map these practices relying on cartographic tools. Digital methods, including geo-mapping, have allowed us to visualize evolving behavioral patterns over time and space (Bagheri 2014; Caragea et al. 2014; Kristensen 2015; Pickles 2012; Torres and Costa 2014). Current geospatial data analysis software integrates a multitude of datasets, creating various data layers on a digital map. As a result, it is able to visualize data that is not only geocoded, but it also provides complementary details on the context, conditions, and the area in question, including demographic information for the analyzed locations. In the context of LGBTQ struggles

DOI: 10.4324/9781003565871-4

evoked, multi-layered mapmaking represents a valuable resource to capture the synergies between different LGBTQ communities across geographic regions and increase the visibility of these trends.

Virtual Mapmaking and (In)Visibility

One of the basic tenets of quantitative research is the ability to aggregate data in view of generalizability (Haig 2018). However, generalizable trends do not necessarily promote a deeper understanding of complex social justice processes. The invaluable insights of rich case studies combined with comparative case analysis have led to rich and multilayered analyses. Innovative data visualization technology and geo-mapping tools in humanistic social sciences enable researchers to unearth dynamic interactions between actors, contexts, and conditions while maintaining detailed local case study data. Past research emphasizes the importance of work on alternative justice mechanisms to complement and contextualize insights from existing traditional literature (Belhadj and Kurze 2021; Kurze 2016, 2019, 2020). Below, we introduce a large *n* case study to capture and map global LGBTQ collaboration across different geographic regions during the post-Arab Spring era, notably focusing on synergies among different LGBTQ communities within the Global South.

Despite our ability to capture less visible phenomena thanks to technological advances, we are conscious of limitations associated with mapmaking. Engaging in cartography requires being aware of underlying power relations when drawing maps (Crampton and Krygier 2018). Critical cartography rose to prominence in the 1990s, criticizing power imbalances native to the craft. Recent debates have questioned the potential of emancipatory power in the field (Kim 2015, 216). According to Annette Kim, the immediate subjects of a mapping project should ideally be integrated into the process (Kim 2015, 216). Efforts to capture truth-seeking initiatives across the United States illustrate the challenges associated with grounding work in knowledge, experience and representation.[2] The mapping output for this chapter embraces a holistic perspective that "sets out a roadmap for readers, drawing attention to the landmarks" and helping situate the work in a broader scholarly context (Basu, Kirby, and Shepherd 2020, 2). By focusing on marginalized actors and disclosing less visible themes, we shed light on "new contestations, tensions and constellations of power," reframing the politics of justice (Basu, Kirby, and Shepherd 2020, 2).

Map Design and Data Limitations

This cartographic visualization captures some of the struggles mentioned in Chapter 1, concentrating on specific LGBTQ community practices to fuel cross-national and cross-regional collaborations. Our exploratory cartographic analysis focuses on a handful of separate categories of mechanisms. It compares various forms of justice-oriented engagements to establish a voice or greater visibility, including activism, lobbying, advocacy, and art-related activities. The data for this analysis was retrieved from publicly available on-line sources, since the post-Arab Spring era. The date and location for each collected incident were recorded for visualization purposes. Multiple loca-tions per incident were possible to indicate collaboration between multiple actors across multiple sites. The current data selection includes 38 data entries across Latin America, Africa, and the Middle East and North Africa (MENA) region and Asia, particularly focusing on synergies across the Global South.

Some initial limitations include issues inherent to source materials, data se-lection, and visualization tools. The data sources were not homogenous and re-quired manual coding for event type and actor type. Furthermore, the dataset is part of an ongoing project that will be expanded to provide more homogenous data point comparisons and a larger, uniform database structure. Some collabo-rations include indirect or direct involvement of Global North partners. Due to local partners' ownership, they were included in the current dataset. The data source carries other limitations. Data sources only include publicly available information, overlooking many localized practices by grassroots organizations and individual LGBTQ community members. Only newsworthy stories appear on institutional websites and blogs, rendering less newsworthy activities invis-ible. Some of these issues have been remedied in the ongoing data collection and curation of the interactive map, which also integrates interview data from participants across the Global South. Last, although the selected data visualiza-tion software offers a variety of functions, we performed limited mapping for this geo-mapping output. Additional coding with more nuanced categories of practices, actors, locations and time periods offers room for future interpreta-tion and complementary data analysis of the original study design.

The Mapmaking, Challenges, and Takeaways

The exploratory cartography was performed with ArcGIS Online and up-loaded on a publicly accessible server.[3] ArcGIS Online is a server-based soft-ware for geo-mapping and data-driven visualization of multiple layers in a single map. The current maps provide viewers with a topography of various stakeholders engaged in these processes as well as an initial sketch of the dif-ferent types of activities they are engaged in. The maps contain data from the post-Arab Spring until the present. The current visualization includes pop-ups for each incident, allowing viewers to click on locations on the map and learn more about the actors and type of event and the time of occurrence. The ob-jective of this interactive map is to provide an overview of LGBTQ practices from a comparative perspective notably, but not exclusively across the Global South. The present maps aggregate incidents and visualize event frequency across different engagement categories, including activism, lobbying, advo-cacy, litigation, and art-related activities.

Initial Topography of Stakeholders and Activities

An exploratory compilation and codification of data show a large variety of stakeholders within the LGBTQ communities across different world regions. For our first map, we color coordinated different types of actors within several world regions, including Latin America, Africa, the MENA region, and Asia. The map shows that the range of actors engaging in LGBTQ issues does not solely include stakeholders explicitly advocating for causes directly relating to sexual minorities (labeled under LGBTQ advocacy in Figure 2.1). In fact, often, the sociopolitical context does not allow for actors to directly engage with these topics, sometimes because of the prohibition of homosexuality, at times because of the cultural and normative environment, or both. Interestingly, nongovernmental organizations that work in the medical field, public health and well-being, and gender inclusion, all feature among LGBTQ community allies depending on the country-specific context. Artists and media organizations are also among important actors in certain cases. More often than not different actor constellations coalesce and collaborate across a variety of topics and issues. In subsequent visualizations one of the goals lies in further teasing out the intertwined nature of some of these collaborations and highlighting it in an interactive map feature online. The exploratory mapping efforts, however, underscore more direct LGBTQ activities across Latin America and slightly more NGO-related work in areas of the MENA region and parts of Asia. Additional analysis, such as frequency and time series may provide compelling insights on these trends within a region as well as across regions and remain to be performed in the next phase of the project.

This map represents an initial capture and visualization of LGBTQ collaborations across the Global South and contains several limitations for broader public use and with regard to generalizability. First, the dataset is limited to a total of 38 cases across three regions, including some overlapping cases based on different partnerships of LGBTQ communities. Consequently, the current map is a call to further explore and capture the emergence and existence of LGBTQ collaborations across the Global South across geographic locations and across time. More refined searches and the inclusion of other data sources, such as archival material, interview data and additional social media elements will help further understand the nuances between a variety of engagements in different contexts and time periods. In sum, however, these exploratory results—particularly with regard to capturing the existence of art-inspired collaborations—have illustrated the extent to which different stakeholders have engaged publicly considering different events.

For our second map (Figure 2.2), we color coordinated different types of activities within the different regional areas. The activity categories were defined as follows. First, LGBTQ advocacy, which directly involves references to sexual minorities and their needs. Second, human rights activism, which presents LGBTQ causes less explicitly, emphasizes the general rights and

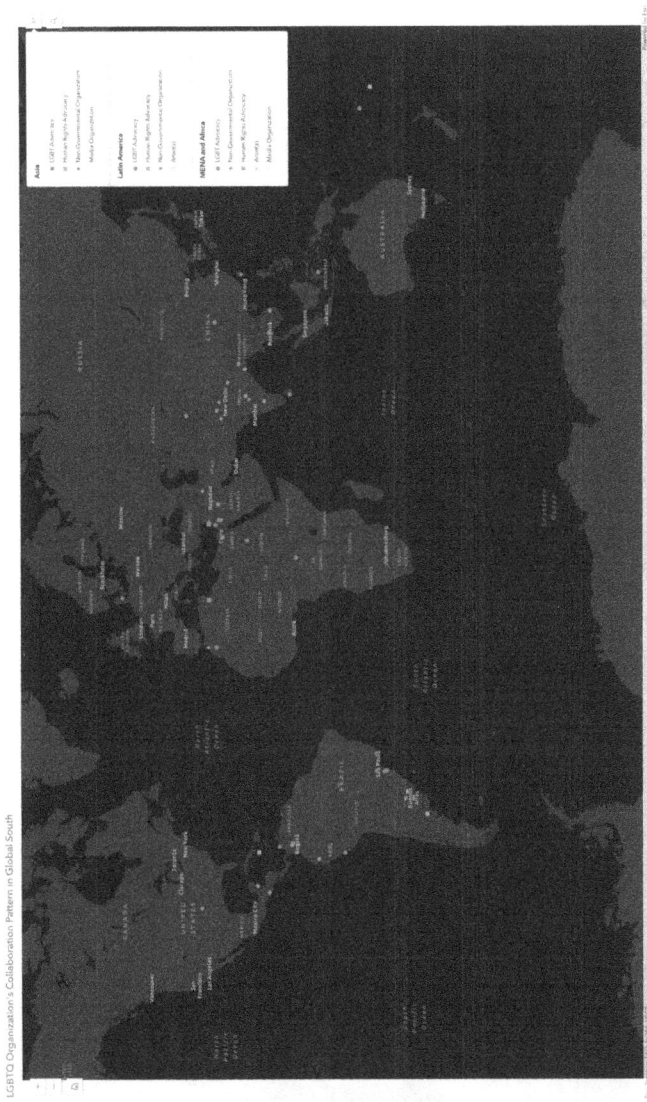

Figure 2.1 Map visualization of different LGBTQ organization types collaborating across the Global South. Created by authors.

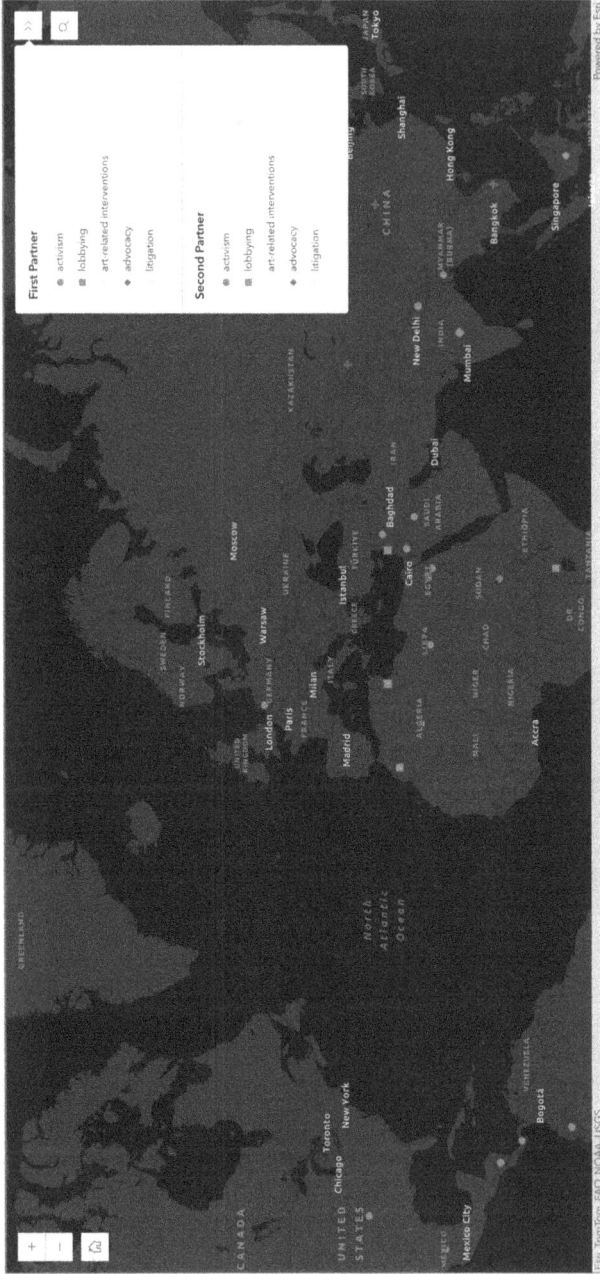

Figure 2.2 Map visualization of different types of LGBTQ collaborations across the Global South. Created by authors.

norms culture around human rights (for various reasons). While the lobbying category mainly represents legal reform efforts led by LGBTQ activists and allies, the advocacy label on the map refers to activities that go beyond policy-related agenda setting, including workshops and normative changes at the societal level through awareness campaigns and other activities. Litigation directly uses the judicial system and existing laws to promote LGBTQ issues. Art-inspired practices have become a staple choice of action in certain contexts and often occur at the intersection of issues, including queerness, gender and race.

Data Mapping and Visualization Following Case Study Analyses

While the brunt of our book delves into a variety of case studies in following Chapters 3–7, Chapter 8 presents a meta-analysis drawing from the methodological insights discussed in this chapter. Instead of providing a global map of subversive collective action across different countries and regions, the goal is to offer our readers a selection of visualizations of country-specific data to gain better insights of a variety of trends and issues in view of different sexual minorities across these cases. More precisely, Chapter 8 is framed by a typology of subversive activities, drawing from the experiences of LGBTQ advocates in the MENA region, Russia, and Singapore. The analysis underscores the resilience and adaptability of queer activism in the face of systemic oppression, providing researchers, scholars, advocates, practitioners, and students with a valuable tool for furthering understanding and advocacy.

As for the MENA region and the so-called spaces of otherness (briefly mentioned in Chapter 1), the following Chapters 3 and 4 explore the creation of alternative spaces for sexual minorities in the MENA region, focusing on the roles of social media and collective action during political transitions. Using Foucauldian concepts of heterotopia, the chapters highlight how LGBTQ activists in Tunisia and Lebanon navigate and create new spaces for deliberation and identity formation. Both chapters emphasize the fragile nature of these spatialities, challenged by secularist and Islamist traditions. Art emerges as a critical medium for queer activism, facilitating innovative spaces for dialogue and resistance. The meta-analysis in Chapter 8 draws from these insights to map the various forms of subversive activities, including digital activism and cultural interventions, that characterize LGBTQ advocacy in the MENA region. The case study on Singapore, which centers on neocolonial legacies and queerness, examines how queer advocacy unfolds within a restrictive yet economically prosperous and stable environment. The chapter outlines the non-confrontational modes of LGBTQ activism, shaped by the state's commitment to pragmatic values and security. By conducting narrative interviews with local activists, the chapter reveals how these advocates strategically define their roles amidst cultural polarization and neocolonial tensions. The meta-analysis in Chapter 8 incorporates Singapore's case to highlight how integration and alignment, rather than direct confrontation, can serve as effective strategies for consolidating queer acceptance in restrictive contexts. The last meta-analysis in Chapter 8 focuses on Russia's queer scapegoating and underground activism, illustrating the complex interplay between political repression and queer resilience. In fact, our Russia chapter (Chapter 7) delves into the repressive political strategies employed by the Russian regime, particularly the scapegoating of LGBTQ communities to divert attention from internal issues and maintain social order. The chapter maps the increased persecution and state-condoned violence against queer individuals, forcing activism into an underground mode of operation. The resilience of Russian LGBTQ activists, who adopt covert strategies to avoid state persecution, is a testament to the adaptability required in such hostile environments.

Integrative Framework and Cross-Regional Insights

The meta-analysis presented in Chapter 8 integrates these diverse case studies, offering a holistic framework for understanding the daily struggles of LGBTQ communities in repressive settings. By outlining a typology of subversive activities, the chapter provides a detailed map of the strategies and responses employed by queer advocates in the MENA region, Russia, and Singapore. The chapter emphasizes the importance of a cross-disciplinary, intersectional approach in furthering research and advocacy, highlighting the interconnectedness of global LGBTQ struggles. Rather than prescribing a one-size-fits-all blueprint, the chapter underscores the need for contextual sensitivity and adaptability in queer activism. The reflections and insights offered here serve as an inspiration for continued efforts toward equality and justice, encouraging researchers and advocates to explore new avenues for supporting LGBTQ rights in diverse and challenging environments. Using geo-mapping and data visualization, this chapter aims to provide a deeper understanding of the resilience and innovation that define queer activism worldwide.

Conclusion

This chapter aimed at introducing a critical perspective on alternative spaces for emancipation within LGBTQ communities across various regions of the Global South. The term critical applies here in two ways. First, from a theoretical perspective by introducing spatial studies to LGBTQ issues within the context of the Global South. Second, in terms of applied mixed methods to process empirical data on the issue. In fact, the digital visualization of synergies and collaborative efforts among different stakeholders using ArcGIS constitutes an initial effort to visually and tangibly illustrate alliances and transnational and cross-regional work of LGBTQ advocacy groups and LGBTQ allies. Certes, this exploratory work will benefit from further expanding the number of cases and additional data that includes a larger number of countries, regions and collaborative activities. In addition, it would also benefit from crowdsourcing. In other words, create an open-source platform that allows for researchers, stakeholders and interested individuals or groups to add data, all of which is currently being evaluated and examined. Interview data will be integrated in the next phase of the mapping project, which consists of narrative-style visualizations. Some limitations apply here as well, notably with regard to protecting the privacy and identities of research participants and local stakeholders.

Moreover, against the backdrop of recent Queer Theory literature and postcolonial legacies, we used spatial concepts, particularly the idea of in-between spaces, to highlight the varying trends of LGBTQ stakeholders in different contexts and areas to promote justice and create greater visibility for marginalized and oppressed communities. Empowering local communities, however, is associated with intricate challenges and the exploratory maps provide an excellent opportunity to showcase some of these activities in a concise and more tangible way.

To continue to complete the existing data, we also seek to integrate interview data from community members across different regions, creating narrative-style storytelling that is embedded in the virtual online maps. As such, the goal is to create a living online document that is publicly available, which continues to tell the story of important strides to tackle injustice and marginalization of lesser visible groups and individuals from a transnational and cross-regional perspective. Despite remaining challenges and obstacles, including notably the safety and well-being of LGBTQ community members, current and past engagements and activities have proven that the time is in favor of transformative change, including research, the harnessing of online spaces and the continued collaboration of stakeholders across professions and disciplines. The lessons learned from geo-mapping the engagement of specific queer communities across various regions serve as a stepping stone for our mapping-focused analysis of some of our case study findings. Next, we continue with exploring a variety of case studies in the chapters to follow.

Notes

1 This section draws from original ideas first published in (Balasco et al. 2022).
2 See for instance the interactive map by the Mary Hoch Center for Reconciliation at George Mason University, https://www.mapcustomizer.com/map/US%20Truth%20and%20Reconciliation%20Initiatives%202020, accessed 25 June 2021.
3 The interactive maps are available online. A map capturing the different types of organizations is available here https://montclair.maps.arcgis.com/apps/instant/basic/index.html?appid=6e6429c5de504914a9f4ffc8123fe4f2. A map categorizing the different types of activities can be seen here, https://montclair.maps.arcgis.com/apps/instant/basic/index.html?appid=f385b97dbcaa4f508e9b53de1b8bcace, accessed 4 June 2024.

References

Bagheri, Nazgol. 2014. "Mapping Women in Tehran's Public Spaces: A Geo-Visualization Perspective." *Gender, Place and Culture: A Journal of Feminist Geography* 21 (10): 1285–301.

Balasco, Lauren, Bea Ciordia, Eliza Garnsey, Sarine Karajerjian, Arnaud Kurze, Christopher K. Lamont, Nomzamo Ntombela, and Mariam Salehi. 2022. "Introducing Justicecraft: Political Change Across Space and Time." *Political Anthropological Research on International Social Sciences (PARISS)* 3 (1): 51–108.

Basu, S., P. Kirby, and L. J. Shepherd. 2020. "Women, Peace and Security: A Critical Cartography." In *New Directions in Women, Peace and Security*, edited by Soumita Basu, Paul Kirby, and Laura J. Shepherd, 1–18. Bristol: Bristol University Press.

Belhadj, Aymen, and Arnaud Kurze. 2021. "Whose Justice? Youth, Reconciliation and the State in Post-Ben Ali Tunisia." *Journal of Human Rights* 20 (3): 356–72.

Caragea, Cornelia, Anna Cinzia Squicciarini, Sam Stehle, Kishore Neppalli, Andrea H. Tapia, and Others. 2014. "Mapping Moods: Geo-Mapped Sentiment Analysis during Hurricane Sandy." In *ISCRAM*. Citeseer. https://citeseerx.ist.psu.edu/viewdoc/download?doi=10.1.1.432.8700&rep=rep1&type=pdf.

Crampton, Jeremy W., and Jonh Krygier. 2018. "An Introduction to Critical Cartography," November. http://beu.extension.unicen.edu.ar/xmlui/handle/123456789/359.

Haig, Brian D. 2018. *The Philosophy of Quantitative Methods*. Oxford: Oxford University Press.

Kim, Annette M. 2015. "Critical Cartography 2.0: From 'participatory Mapping' to Authored Visualizations of Power and People." *Landscape and Urban Planning* 142 (October):215–25.

Kristensen, Peter Marcus. 2015. "Revisiting the 'American Social Science'—Mapping the Geography of International Relations." *International Studies Perspectives* 16 (3): 246–69.

Kurze, Arnaud. 2016. "#WarCrimes #PostConflictJustice #Balkans: Youth, Performance Activism and the Politics of Memory." *The International Journal of Transitional Justice* 10 (3): 451–70.

Kurze, Arnaud. 2019. "Youth Activism, Art, and Transitional Justice." In *New Critical Spaces in Transitional Justice: Gender, Art, and Memory*, edited by Arnaud Kurze and Christopher Lamont, 63–85. Bloomington, IN: Indiana University Press.

Kurze, Arnaud. 2020. "Seeking New Metaphors: Gender Identities in Tunisia and Lebanon." In *Arab Spring: Modernity, Identity and Change*, edited by Eid Mohamed and Dalia Fahmy, 207–33. Cham: Springer International Publishing.

Pickles, John. 2012. *A History of Spaces: Cartographic Reason, Mapping and the Geo-Coded World*. Abingdon: Routledge.

Torres, Yuri Queiroz Abreu, and Lucia Maria Sá Antunes Costa. 2014. "Digital Narratives: Mapping Contemporary Use of Urban Open Spaces through Geo-Social Data." *Procedia Environmental Sciences* 22 (January):1–11.

Part 2

Struggles in Contested Queer Spaces

The second part includes five chapters offering detailed case studies from different regions. Chapter 3 delves into the creation of alternative spaces for sexual minorities during political transitions, with an emphasis on social media and collective action in the Middle East and North Africa. Chapter 4 investigates how art functions as a medium to establish innovative spaces for deliberation amid political stagnation or regression, particularly in Tunisia and Lebanon. Chapter 5 explores non-confrontational approaches to LGBTQ activism within a pragmatic and postcolonial framework, focusing on Singapore. Chapter 6 examines the evolution of queer activism in an illiberal context, highlighting the impact of student activism and the creation of refugee spaces in Poland. Chapter 7 addresses the repressive politics in autocratic regimes and the resilience-driven underground queer activism in Russia.

DOI: 10.4324/9781003565871-5

3   Spaces of Otherness Across the Middle East and North Africa[1]

"Across the Middle East, LGBTQ communities face a growing crackdown [...] to restrict the rights of gay and transgender people and erase their influence from society," writes Mohamad El Chamaa in the *Washington Post* in 2023 (El Chamaa 2023). This chapter traces some of the more recent trends, providing not only an empirical snapshot across different country cases, but also a conceptual framing to better understand the struggles faced by sexual and gender minorities in these contexts.

Over a decade after popular uprisings across the MENA region sparked hope for cautious democratic transitions (Mansfield and Snyder 2012), the state of democratic gains and human rights progress for sexual and gender minorities is bleak. A report by Human Rights Watch deplores the repressive trends by governments across the region, e.g. entrapping LGBT people on social media and dating applications, often subjecting them to online extortion, online harassment, and outings. The report also states that security forces often "relied on illegitimately obtained digital photos, chats, and similar information in prosecutions, in violation of the right to privacy and other human rights" (Younes 2023). These resurging trends are not new, but a continuation of past efforts to stifle alternative voices and political and social integration of these minority groups.

On 4 January 2016, almost five years after the youth-propelled ouster of President Zine El Abdine Ben Ali, the festivities to celebrate the anniversary of a new era in Tunisian society were overshadowed by a court sentence to suspend the activities of Shams, an organization working to support sexual and gender minorities.[2] The celebrations were also tainted by a high number of police and security checkpoints as a result of the extremist violence in prior months at the Bardo Museum in Tunis, at a hotel in Sousse and against the presidential guard, which led to a heightened alertness and the extension of emergency laws. Although Shams appealed the verdict and won its case, the "securitization of democracy" against the backdrop of extremism, a sluggish economy, and political opposition from Islamists continues to affect civil rights and democratic consolidation in the country (Kurze 2018). And despite an openly gay candidate during the 2019 presidential elections (Lyman and

DOI: 10.4324/9781003565871-6

Khatib 2019), discrimination of LGBTQ members continues. Queer spaces in Tunisian society oscillate between watchful state institutions—with the judiciary cracking down on LGBTQ minorities ("Tunisia" 2024)—and civil society organizations, such as the Association for Justice and Equality (Damj), standing up for minority rights and challenging legal decisions and processes (Amnesty International 2023). Despite international efforts to promote LGBTQ rights by the United Nations and the appointment of an LGBTQ watchdog (Smida 2016), Tunisian legislators have yet to decriminalize sodomy laws in place since 1964.

In contrast, also in early 2016, in Lebanon, a Beirut judge delivered a ruling in favor of a transgender individual, who sought to change his gender marker on public records and in the national civil registry (Hafez 2016). This sentence followed an earlier verdict, challenging Article 534 of Lebanon's Penal Code that prohibits sexual relations contradicting the laws of nature (Azzi 2014). The particular verdict rendered the law inapplicable in a case against an intersex-born self-identified woman accused of having an unnatural sexual relationship with a man. Slivers of hope for legal protection of minority rights, however, are clashing with the bleak reality in the streets of the Lebanese capital, a country marked by continued political turmoil and the ongoing civil war in neighboring Syria. Although the Lebanese penal code prescribes up to one-year jail sentences for "sexual intercourse against nature," it is rarely enforced. Advocacy work in Lebanon during the post-Arab Spring era was especially common in urban and cosmopolitan areas, like Beirut. In recent years, however, members of the LGBTQ community have been facing both official and social discrimination and harassment (House 2024).

In Morocco, the legal framework aligns with its neighboring countries, as article 489 of the Penal Code prohibits "lewd or unnatural acts" between individuals of the same sex with a penalty of up to three years imprisonment and a fine (Morocco 2019). The situation for the Moroccan queer community is challenging, notably as the Arab uprisings fell short of social and political change in society (Belghazi and Moudden 2016; Hill 2019; Willis 2014). Arrests by authorities and discrimination are part of the continued struggles faced by sexual minorities as they navigate a legal landscape that offers no protection. According to a country-of-origin report by Danish immigration services, the actual number of arrests is much higher than publicized by the Moroccan authorities.[3]

In 2020, an online harassment campaign surged, aimed at outing men on same-sex dating apps. Users created fake accounts, exposing members of the online community, leading to discriminatory practices, physical harm and ostracized individuals (Reid 2020). Though the perpetrators of a 2022 assault against a trans woman in Tangier were seized by the police, laws against harassment and discrimination do not exist in the country (El Atti - Rabat 2022). Some token celebrities, such as the openly gay writer Abdellah Taïa, however, are also being instrumentalized by different stakeholders for their own means.

In addition, these celebrities generally do not reside in Morocco (Christensen 2017). Some cracks or opportunities in the repressive regime are nonetheless visible, as authorities have tolerated a gay magazine called *Mithly*, created in 2010. As the government has not officially allowed the publication and distribution of the magazine, the production occurs on foreign territory in Spain (Smith 2010). Reminiscent to the Tunisian organization Damj or the Lebanese association Shams, in Morocco, an early LGBTQ organization, Kif-Kif was maneuvering in a legal twilight zone without any official recognition from the government, but was able to promote public health services to its community. Today, there is a renewed grassroots effort with over a dozen organizations working in the trenches, including Nassawiyat, Trans Dynamique, Taanit, and Groupe D'Action Auto Feministe (A. 2024).

In neighboring Algeria, people "know homosexuality exists, but tend to avoid the subject and feel gay people should keep to themselves" (Schembri 2019). Thanks to the transformative power of social media, individual LGBTQ members feel less of an outcast, but may face severe punishment due to the repressive laws still in place in the country. Equaldex, a website that traces the evolution of LGBTQ rights around the world placed Algeria on rank 169 after North Korea, and before Uganda.[4] Algerian law punishes same-sex activity with two months to two years imprisonment and a fine (Article 333). Any same-sex-related activities are also referred to as "outrage to public decency" consisting of "an act against nature with an individual of the same sex" (Article 338), with even steeper jail time up to three years and a fine.[5] In 2020, Algerian authorities conducted a raid arresting over three dozen men at a private gay wedding, against the backdrop of national anti-LGBTQ laws (Younes 2020a). The state is actively blocking the formation of LGBTQ organizations (Younes 2020a), creating little hope for activists engaged in the cause.

Notwithstanding persisting challenges, LGBTQ advocacy is part of a broader democratic movement that swept across the MENA region. "Rather than trying to change public opinion," as Eric Goldstein describes, it is about "mobilizing civil society" (2016). The Arab Spring fell short of many aspired goals, including civil rights advancement, political participation and individual freedoms across the MENA. It demonstrated, however, the inherent strength of youth activism and social movements in these societies. There is a generational and normative shift slowly transforming current social structures. The median age of Algeria's population is 28 years, 30 years in Lebanon and Morocco and 31 for Tunisia.[6] According to the World Bank close to two-thirds of the population in the MENA are under the age of 30 (Khan 2018). While statistical data indicates that society is composed of a vast young generation of citizens, Tunisia is led by old elites, often well into their eighties. This, in turn, creates a generational disconnect. The generational fault lines do not run as deep in Lebanon, but political struggles fueled by sectarian politics and old power elites have also sidelined youth from national politics (Szekely

2015). As for Morocco, the political structures draw on legitimation that consists of "a threefold structure combining religion, nationalism and a monarchy or hereditary rule," with the King, Mohammed VI, oscillating between power brokerage and alliance building but resting on its deep-rooted grip (Naguib 2020, 408). And in Algeria, despite the ouster of long-term President Bouteflika in 2019, the military continues to exert tremendous influence despite the civilian appearance of the political apparatus (Oumansour 2019).

Consequently, youth activists' ambitions for transformative change have shifted from the political to the social and cultural levels. This book analyzes the emergence and challenges of disseminating normative, identity-driven narratives in times of transition. Yet it draws on a concept of youth that goes beyond the legal notion of adulthood that defines youth as minors below a certain age.[7] Instead, we embrace a more culturally inspired model that describes youth as an experience that shapes the individual's level of dependency. The level of dependency is often contingent on economic factors and emotional ties to the youth's family (Furlong 2012). Focusing on a wide range of youth actors in their twenties and thirties, the following chapters analyze the emergence of collective identities, particularly non-normative sexualities in societies. Shifting the research focus from institutional politics to contested spaces of social norms doesn't remove politics from the analytical equation. On the contrary, it emphasizes the politicization of moral sexual high grounds in these societies. It also sheds light on institutional and normative gray areas during social transformation processes.

Given the unyielding, repressive politics across the MENA region, the authors explore the question of why and how the respective LGBTQ communities were able to consolidate their human rights advances despite the official and social challenges. The following chapter maps different types of collective action and related activities to illustrate how during this process, art served as a medium to create innovative spaces of deliberation. The authors selected two case studies, Lebanon and Tunisia, as a deliberate choice for comparison, despite their sociopolitical and cultural differences. The emergence of a broader, public LGBTQ narrative in both contexts, however, offers an excellent opportunity for a closer examination by relying on John Stuart Mill's method of difference, which will further be elaborated on in the methodology section (Lijphart 1975).

Here, we provide a conceptual framework to better situate and contextualize the conditions and activities. We draw on Foucault's concept of heterotopia—spaces of otherness that are simultaneously physical and mental—to present new findings on the difficulties connected to generating spaces of collective identity and shared narratives. The conceptual grounding helps better understand the role of art, social media and the impact of social movements to address human rights abuses. This is crucial, as the creation of this new fragile spatiality is challenged by several factors, including narratives and memories of secularist and sectarian traditions.

LGBTQ Rights and Spaces of "Otherness" during Transitions

While both LGBTQ rights and the concept of space are essential in the transitional contexts, they have been under-studied. The notion of space has found extensive academic attention notably in sociology as well as post-structuralist and postmodern debates. As seen in Chapter 1, Pierre Bourdieu and Michel Foucault grappled with the creation, appropriation and evolution of space. While the former uses the term field to denote the context and social milieu in which individuals and social groups interact (Bourdieu 1985), Foucault discusses the concept of space by juxtaposing geography, knowledge and power (Crampton and Elden 2007). He illustrates the power struggle between different stakeholders by analyzing the relationship between place and being. His focus on a physical location, such as a prison, contextualizes its broader sociopolitical and philosophical impact on society (see, for instance, M. Foucault 1977).

When grappling with past human rights violations, various authors have also employed the concept of space to address several questions associated with the difficulties of dealing with the past. For instance, the notions of public space and victims' voices are frequent recurring tropes in the literature. Based on a gender perspective, some authors describe the relentless efforts of civil society to create a public space for victims' groups "to tell their truths and be heard" (Crosby and Lykes 2011). Their case exemplifies the empowerment of a voiceless group. In the case of post-Ben-Ali Tunisia, the gender initiative by the International Center for Transitional Justice (ICTJ) is an excellent example that underlines the efforts of creating a voice for marginalized groups within society.[8]

Although past research has centered around notions of accountability and empowerment of social actors, questions about the creation of alternative spaces during transition periods and the visibility and recognition of repressed groups remain in the dark (see, for instance, Kurze 2019a). This chapter addresses these shortcomings by laying the conceptual framework to better understand the struggles of Tunisian and Lebanese LGBTQ communities during times of transition discussed in Chapter 4. Both the aftermath of the Cedar and the Jasmine Revolutions provided LGBTQ activists with an opportunity to gain momentum to establish civil and human rights for sexual minorities amidst a changing political and institutional landscape. Although the empirical case studies about the challenges of LGBTQ advocacy in our book demonstrate that the efforts for equality are only at the beginning, our book helps expand a growing literature. While we address the broader question of queer spaces and religion notably in Chapter 6, homosexuality and Islam have found scholarly attention since the sexual liberation in the postmodern world (El-Rouayheb 2009; Habib 2007). These initial works paved the road for interdisciplinary research including the fields of sexuality studies, religious studies and cultural studies. More recently, Amanullah De Sondy explored the social construct of masculinity within Islam. Drawing from a case study on the Quran and Pakistan, he argues that the rigidity of the concept results in secularization and alienation of those who cannot identify with the narrow definition of traditions and social behaviors associated with it. He states that "theocratic Islamists idealize entrenched masculinity defined through familial dominance and shows of power, sometimes expressed as militarism. The rigidity of the masculinity that emerges prompts a certain exodus from religious Islam" (De Sondy 2014, 1).

Some of these power struggles are particularly visible during the post-Arab Spring transitions. Tunisia serves as an excellent case in point. The country was built on a French secular institutional model, when the first President Habib Bourguiba led the nation to its independence from its French colonizer in 1956. Notwithstanding, Islam features as the country's religion in the constitution.[9] When Ennahda, the Islamist party, won the 2011 elections, its leaders gave this constitutional prerogative a new political meaning that would help buttress the party's power structures within society. The rising tensions from 2011 to 2014 between secular and religious forces —especially between human rights activists and conservative religious groups—are exemplary. During the Printemps des Art 2012, an international art and culture festival in the capital Tunis, for instance, Salafists devastated an exhibit with paintings and sculptures promoting feminism and freedom of artistic expression (Kurze 2019b). Images and concepts of sexuality and gender were at the center of the clashes. As De Sondy rightly notes, "Gender is constructed through a series of reflections with the other, including other men and women. Such a dynamic creates, and constructs gender based on power with catastrophic consequences, at times involving killing and bloodshed" (De Sondy 2014, 180).

Morocco's queer spaces have also been at the center of heated debates, particularly showcasing the tensions between physical, virtual and social spaces. In 2020, a transgender Moroccan activist, Sofia Talouni, living in Turkey started a campaign encouraging the outing of closeted gay people in Morocco, which resulted in numerous reported cases of harassment and death threats against LGBTQ people (Ale-Ebrahim 2023). By mapping a series of contentious politics of LGBTQ supporters, the objective of our book lies in raising awareness to understudied issues of acknowledging sexual minorities in post-conflict and post-authoritarian regimes. Today, for instance, discrimination and prosecution against sexual minorities continue and remain of concern highlighted in various human rights reports (Amnesty International 2023; "Tunisia" 2024; Younes 2020b).

Issues pertaining to sexual minorities in the Arab world are not new and have found scholarly attention (Khalaf and Gagnon 2006). The creation of queer spaces in urban, metropolitan areas, such as Beirut, is telling and can be described as the creation of "urban sites that foster attempts, not necessarily always with success, at transcending spatio-temporal fixities" (Merabet

2006). These boundaries, however, led to the emergence of different groups of homosexuals in post-civil war Lebanon, instead of generating a unified community (Merabet 2006). Navigating a small hostile space with little prospect of anonymity for safety reasons, led to dispersed queer islands across the city (Merabet 2006). Furthermore, gay and lesbian relations were tense given the patriarchal history of the country. Since the new millennium, Lebanon has experienced a growing gay social scene and "gay men who are not only openly gay but defend their 'lifestyle' with a more audible voice" (McCormick 2006). James McCormick illustrates how these men contest traditional social constructs of masculinity and negotiate their identities in an increasingly globalized and interconnected society.

Some have observed similar trends across various urban metropolises across the Arab world and the MENA region, including Israel (Hartal and Misgav 2021; Misgav and Hartal 2019). Drawing on the notion of spaces, Matthew Gagné, for instance, explores the pre-civil war cityscapes of Damascus in Syria (Saleh 2020). He focuses on the "streets, parks, bars, cafes and hammams where men congregate" (Gagné 2016, 183). As the panoply of spaces which "border one another, not physically, but conceptually and socially," he writes that these "borders are sets of abutting differences of queer bodies and practices that interconnect within a mapping of queer landscape" (Gagné 2016, 183). His attention thus centers on queer geographies and identities, in line with McCormicks contribution. Contrary to these works, Joseph Massad criticizes local agencies as a result of the "Gay International," which he defines as the "missionary tasks, the discourse that produces them, and the organizations that represent them," including international bodies such as the International Lesbian and Gay Association (ILGA) and the International Gay and Lesbian Human Rights Commission (IGLHRC), founded in 1978 and 1991 respectively (Massad 2007, 161). In fact, Gay International promotes a universalist LGBTQ discourse that seeks to transform Arab and Muslim "practitioners of same-sex contact into subjects who identify as 'homosexual' and 'gay'" (Massad 2007, 162). This debate highlights the problematic character of globalizing ideologies and lifestyles that transcend domestic borders and local cultures. It also underlines the dynamic character of the creation of space during transition processes that is not only contested by antagonistic groups, but also questioned by members from within the same community, as its members seek to imagine and forge a common identity for the group (Anderson 1991).

Repression of human rights and minorities in transitional contexts, however, is not only an ideological issue between international and domestic actors but can also be found in the institutional structures of a country in transition. As Tazreena Sajjad demonstrates, major pitfalls include weak governance, deprioritization of the rule of law, burdensome multidimensional coordination and the issue of institutional trust and popularity with the local population (Sajjad 2009). She argues that these obstacles fuel critical debates around these contentious spaces that are continuously renegotiated by those involved. "Rather than disengaging from the question of accountability, the focus should be on how to enhance the capacity and the resources of such institutions so that they can negotiate these narrow spaces even more effectively" (Sajjad 2009, 444). The need to clearly define the role of a contested space by actors involved in transition processes is a common phenomenon in times of political change. Our book homes in on a variety of political and social transitions across different spaces and during time.

Suffice it to say that the politicization of these different identities is poised to affect the perception of the imaginary and the physical space. The above case studies exemplify the number of challenges inherent to transition processes. They particularly emphasize the contentious character of efforts to create new spaces or to redefine existing sites that an emerging group of actors aims to establish and claim their identity. To explore the creation of alternative spaces in the cases of Tunisia and Lebanon, in the next chapter. Here, we draw on Foucault's notion of heterotopia, spaces of otherness. Foucault juxtaposes them to utopias, which are imaginary and do not exist as a real place. According to him, in contrast to utopias,

> There are also, probably in every culture, in every civilization, real places –
> places that do exist and that are formed in the very founding of society –
> which are something like counter-sites, a kind of effectively enacted utopia
> in which the real sites, all the other real sites that can be found within the
> culture, are simultaneously represented, contested, and inverted. Places of
> this kind are outside of all places, even though it may be possible to indi-
> cate their location in reality. Because these places are absolutely different
> from all the sites that they reflect and speak about, I shall call them, by way
> of contrast to utopias, heterotopias
>
> (Michel Foucault 1986, 24).

Foucault's unfinished work on *heterotopias* provides an excellent starting point to examine the creation and appropriation of post-revolutionary space by Tunisian youth and Lebanese activists.[10] It includes individual acts of defiance, such as by a Tunisian youth activist, Amina Sboui, a women's rights activist, who posted a topless picture of herself on Facebook during the March 2013 protests in honor of an assassinated opposition leader. We will look more closely into some of these stories and experiences in the following chapter. It raises a number of questions: Is it merely a mirror of current sociopolitical conditions, a "counter-site" as defined by Foucault, with the aim of resisting the current political struggle (Michel Foucault 1986, 22)? Or do these efforts constitute more than just a form of resistance, creating an alternative space for particular social groups in Tunisian and Lebanese societies as posited by some scholars who further interpreted Foucault's work, drawing on different case studies (Hetherington 1997, viii). To answer these questions, it is important to map a variety of activities by advocacy groups in post-Ben Ali Tunisia and Lebanon's post-Cedar Revolution era. A closer analysis will help distinguish several forms of collective action to establish alternative spaces that contest the status quo and help claim group identities in Tunisian and Lebanese societies.

Conclusion

The next chapter explores the heterotopic landscape by exploring the daily struggles of two cases, Tunisian and Lebanese LGBTQ communities. It accentuates the fluid nature of the imaginary and the virtually tangible spaces between the online world and the streets during times of transition or continued repression. The subsequent chapters focus on Asian and Central European to underscore the transversal character of daily queer struggles. While otherness may ostracize individuals and groups, it provides a physical or imagined ground to create spaces for members of dispersed queer communities to claim their voices, greater visibility, despite backlashes, and recognition.

Notes

1 The concept of spaces of otherness and queer communities was first published as a chapter in an edited volume (Kurze 2020).
2 Shams registered as an association with the government's secretary general in May 2015.
3 See report at https://us.dk/media/9952/coi_report_morocco_protection_assistance_victims_of_human_trafficking_oct_2019.pdf, accessed 7 April, 2024.
4 See Equaldex website at https://www.equaldex.com/region/algeria, accessed 17 April 2024.
5 Ibid
6 See United Nations world demographic data at http://unstats.un.org/, accessed 10 April 2024.
7 In many societies around the world this is eighteen.
8 Interview with ICTJ staff on 13 January 2015.
9 See https://www.wipo.int/wipolex/en/text/498913 accessed 17 April 2024.
10 Foucault wrote his piece "Of Other Spaces" in 1967, for a lecture in Tunisia. It was eventually published before his death in the mid-1980s.

References

Ale-Ebrahim, Benjamin. 2023. "Making Visible the Unseen Queer: Gay Dating Apps and Ideologies of Truthmaking in an Outing Campaign in Morocco." In *The Palgrave Handbook of Gender, Media and Communication in the Middle East and North Africa*, edited by Loubna H. Skalli and Nahed Eltantawy, 31–47. Cham: Springer International Publishing.
Amnesty International. 2023. "Tunisia: Quash Prison Terms for LGBTI Duo Sentenced on Charges of Homosexuality." Amnesty International. February 19. https://www.amnesty.org/en/latest/news/2023/02/tunisia-quash-prison-terms-for-lgbti-duo-sentenced-on-charges-of-homosexuality/

Anderson, Benedict. 1991. *Imagined Communities: Reflections on the Origin and Spread of Nationalism*. London: Verso.

A., Sanae. 2024. "Emergence, Resilience, and Tensions: A Decade of LGBTQ Activism in Morocco." *Arab Reform Initiative*, February. https://www.arab-reform.net/pdf/?pid=30213&plang=en&pcat=.

Azzi, Georges. 2014. "Lebanon's LGBT Community Is Still Suffering Abuses." *NOW*, August 25. https://now.mmedia.me/lb/en/reportsfeatures/561407-more-needs-to-be-done-to-protect-the-rights-of-lebanons-lgbt-community

Belghazi, Taieb, and Abdelhay Moudden. 2016. "Ihbat: Disillusionment and the Arab Spring in Morocco." *The Journal of North African Studies* 21 (1): 37–49.

Bourdieu, Pierre. 1985. "The Genesis of the Concepts of Habitus and Field." *Sociocriticism* 2 (2): 11–24.

Christensen, Tina Dransfeldt. 2017. "Breaking the Silence: Between Literary Representation and LGBT Activism. Abdellah Taïa as Author and Activist." *Expressions Maghrébines* 16 (1): 107–25.

Crampton, Jeremy W., and Stuart Elden. 2007. *Space, Knowledge and Power: Foucault and Geography*. Farnham: Ashgate Publishing, Ltd.

Crosby, Alison, and M. Brinton Lykes. 2011. "Mayan Women Survivors Speak: The Gendered Relations of Truth Telling in Postwar Guatemala." *International Journal of Transitional Justice* 5 (3): 456–76.

De Sondy, Amanullah. 2014. *The Crisis of Islamic Masculinities*. Bloomsbury: Bloomsbury Academic.

El Atti - Rabat, Basma. 2022. "Four Arrested in Morocco for Physical Assault of Trans Woman." The New Arab. November 14. https://www.newarab.com/news/four-arrested-morocco-physical-assault-trans-woman.

El Chamaa, Mohamad. 2023. "Anti-LGBTQ Backlash Grows across Middle East, Echoing U.S. Culture Wars." *The Washington Post*, August 3. https://www.washingtonpost.com/world/2023/08/03/middle-east-lgbtq-gay-transgender/.

El-Rouayheb, Khaled. 2009. *Before Homosexuality in the Arab-Islamic World, 1500-1800*. 49267th edition. Chicago: University Of Chicago Press.

Foucault, M. 1977. *Discipline and Punish*. Penguin Harmondsworth.

Foucault, Michel. 1986. "Of Other Spaces, Heterotopias." *Architecture, Mouvement, Continuité* 16 (1): 22–27.

Furlong, Andy. 2012. *Youth Studies: An Introduction*. New York: Routledge.

Gagné, Mathew. 2016. "The Many Scenes of Queer Damascus." *The Geographies of Body and Borders* 2 (Winter): 182–99.

Goldstein, Eric. 2016. "Dispatches: LGBT Rights Five Years After the Tunisian Uprising." Human Rights Watch. February 8. https://www.hrw.org/news/2016/02/08/dispatches-lgbt-rights-five-years-after-tunisian-uprising.

Habib, Samar. 2007. *Female Homosexuality in the Middle East: Histories and Representations (Routledge Research in Gender and Society)*. 1st edition. Abingdon: Routledge.

Hafez, Ahmed. 2016. "Ruling Marks a First for Transgender People in Lebanon | Human Rights Campaign." Human Rights Campaign. January 28. http://www.hrc.org/blog/ruling-marks-a-first-for-transgender-people-in-lebanon/

Hartal, Gilly, and Chen Misgav. 2021. "Queer Urban Trauma and Its Spatial Politics: A Lesson from Social Movements in Tel Aviv and Jerusalem." *Urban Studies* 58 (7): 1463–83.

Hetherington, Kevin. 1997. *The Badlands of Modernity: Heterotopia and Social Ordering*. London: Psychology Press.

Hill, J. N. C. 2019. "Authoritarian Resilience and Regime Cohesion in Morocco after the Arab Spring." *Middle Eastern Studies* 55 (2): 276–88.

House, Freedom. 2024. "Lebanon." Freedom House. https://freedomhouse.org/country/lebanon/freedom-world/2024.

Khalaf, Samir, and John H. Gagnon, eds. 2006. *Sexualities in the Arab World*. London: Saqi Books.

Khan, Sabahat. 2018. "MENA's Youth Bulge Is a Regional Security Challenge." The Arab Weekly. April 2. https://thearabweekly.com/menas-youth-bulge-regional-security-challenge.

Kurze, Arnaud. 2018. "State Power, Transitions and Resilience: The Securitization of Democracy in Egypt and Tunisia." In *Arab Revolutions: The Dilemma of Democratic Transformation and Its Mechanisms*, edited by Arab Center for Research and Policy Studies, 445–83. Doha: Doha Institute.

Kurze, Arnaud. 2019a. "New Critical Spaces in Transitional Justice: Gender, Art, and Memory." In *New Critical Spaces in Transitional Justice: Gender, Art, and Memory*, edited by Arnaud Kurze and Christopher Lamont, 63–85. Bloomington, IN: Indiana University Press.

Kurze, Arnaud. 2019b. "Youth Activism, Art and Transitional Justice: Emerging Spaces of Memory after the Jasmine Revolution." In *New Critical Spaces in Transitional Justice: Gender, Art, and Memory*, edited by Arnaud Kurze and Christopher Lamont, 63–85. Bloomington, IN: Indiana University Press.

Kurze, Arnaud. 2020. "Seeking New Metaphors: Gender Identities in Tunisia and Lebanon." In *Arab Spring: Modernity, Identity and Change*, edited by Eid Mohamed and Dalia Fahmy, 207–33. Cham: Springer International Publishing.

Lijphart, Arend. 1975. "II. The Comparable-Cases Strategy in Comparative Research." *Comparative Political Studies* 8 (2): 158–77.

Lyman, John, and Hakim Khatib. 2019. "Mounir Baatour, First Openly Gay Candidate in Tunisia, Is Running for President." July 5. https://intpolicydigest.org/mounir-baatour-first-openly-gay-candidate-in-tunisia-is-running-for-president/

Mansfield, Edward D., and Jack Snyder. 2012. "Democratization and the Arab Spring." *International Interactions* 38 (5): 722–33.

Massad, Joseph. 2007. *Desiring Arabs*. Chicago, IL: University of Chicago Press.

McCormick, Jared. 2006. "Transition Beirut: Gay Identities, Lived Realities." In *Sexualities in the Arab World*, edited by Samir Khalaf and John H. Gagnon, 243–60. London: Saqi Books.

Merabet, Sofian. 2006. "Creating Queer Space in Beirut." In *Sexualities in the Arab World*, edited by Samir Khalaf and John H. Gagnon, Chapter 11. London: Saqi Books.

Misgav, Chen, and Gilly Hartal. 2019. "Queer Urban Movements in Tel Aviv and Jerusalem: A Comparative Discussion." In *Routledge Handbook on Middle East Cities*, 57–74. Abingdon: Routledge.

"Morocco." 2019. Human Dignity Trust. February 8. https://www.humandignitytrust.org/country-profile/morocco/

Naguib, Rabia. 2020. "Legitimacy and 'Transitional Continuity' in a Monarchical Regime: Case of Morocco." *International Journal of Public Administration* 43 (5): 404–24.

Oumansour, Par Brahim. 2019. "Who rules Algeria right now? An analysis on the current state of state [power] and how it is changing after the ousting of President

Bouteflika." Paris: IRIS. September 20. https://www.iris-france.org/140130-who-rules-algeria-right-now-an-analysis-on-the-current-state-of-state-power-and-how-it-is-changing-after-the-ousting-of-president-bouteflika/

Reid, Graeme. 2020. "Morocco: Online Attacks Over Same-Sex Relations." Human Rights Watch. April 27. https://www.hrw.org/news/2020/04/27/morocco-online-attacks-over-same-sex-relations

Sajjad, Tazreena. 2009. "These Spaces in Between: The Afghanistan Independent Human Rights Commission and Its Role in Transitional Justice." *International Journal of Transitional Justice* 3 (3): 424–44.

Saleh, Fadi. 2020. "Queer/Humanitarian Visibility: The Emergence of the Figure of The Suffering Syrian Gay Refugee." *Middle East Critique* 29 (1): 47–67.

Schembri, Rose. 2019. "Being Gay in Algeria." Le Monde Diplomatique. August 1. https://mondediplo.com/2019/08/06algeria

Smida, Ohchr/joseph. 2016. "UN Agrees to Appoint Human Rights Expert on Protection of LGBT." UN News. July 1. https://news.un.org/en/story/2016/07/533692

Smith, David. 2010. "Gay Magazine Launched in Morocco." *The Guardian*, May 20, 2010. https://www.theguardian.com/world/2010/may/20/gay-magazine-launch-morocco-rights

Szekely, Ora. 2015. "The Cost of Avoiding Transitional Justice: The Case of Lebanon." In *Transitional Justice and the Arab Spring*, edited by Kirsten J. Fisher and Robert Stewart, 94–111. Abingdon: Routledge.

"Tunisia." 2024. Human Dignity Trust. March 19. https://www.humandignitytrust.org/country-profile/tunisia/

Willis, Michael J. 2014. "Evolution Not Revolution?: Morocco and the Arab Spring." In *Routledge Handbook of the Arab Spring*, 1st edition, 435–50. Abingdon: Routledge.

Younes, Rasha. 2020a. "Algeria: Mass Convictions for Homosexuality." Human Rights Watch. October 15. https://www.hrw.org/news/2020/10/15/algeria-mass-convictions-homosexuality

Younes, Rasha. 2020b. "Tunisia: Two-Year Sentence for Homosexuality." Human Rights Watch. July 6. https://www.hrw.org/news/2020/07/06/tunisia-two-year-sentence-homosexuality

Younes, Rasha. 2023. "Middle East, North Africa: Digital Targeting of LGBT People." Human Rights Watch. February 21. https://www.hrw.org/news/2023/02/21/middle-east-north-africa-digital-targeting-lgbt-people

4 LGBTQ Communities and Transitions in Tunisia and Lebanon[1]

Let us continue to unpeel the various layers of the heterotopic landscape laid out in the previous chapter by scrutinizing the everyday challenges of Tunisian and Lebanese LGBTQ communities. Both cases, as we illustrate here, underscore the amorphous nature of the spaces created by members of these minority groups. The perennially volatile and uncertain transitional contexts, which these societies are confronted with, paint a gloomy picture of the virtually tangible spaces of the online world. This also extends to the physicality of urban landscapes, including bars, cafes, streets and squares, all of which are a testament of persisting repression and discrimination not only by official authorities, but also by prejudiced norms and practices within society. Although diverging sexual and gender identities may repudiate individuals and groups unfairly and fuel exclusionary spaces, it also serves as a catalyst for spaces, as we will see below, that allow for scattered queer folk to assert their voices, gain more prominence, and, despite facing resistance, achieve acknowledgment. Our subsequent chapters on Asian and Central European experiences continue in a similar vein, further accentuating the transversal character of daily queer struggles under these conditions.

Comparing and contrasting Lebanon and Tunisia here despite their sociopolitical and cultural differences is beneficial as it provides us with a nuanced and varied picture of transitional contexts. The former can be characterized as a "post-conflict case" due to its long and devastating civil war, which lasted from 1975 until 1990. During the difficult postwar transition period the 2005 Cedar Revolution served as a watershed moment in the country's transition when civil society protested Rafiq al-Hariri's assassination forming a nonviolent civil resistance movement. Post-Arab Spring Tunisia, on the contrary, can best be described as a "post-authoritarian regime," without the typical traits of a war-torn country. The post-Ben Ali era therefore constitutes the more recent transition period for the Tunisian case. Drawing on Mill's method of difference, these contrasting contexts manifest sufficient variance on the operative and control variables and hence provide excellent opportunity, because "the most typical kind of research in the field of comparative politics takes place at the macro level: it focuses on the characteristics of systems,

DOI: 10.4324/9781003565871-7

large subsystems, and partial systems" (Lijphart 1975, 165). The emergence of a broader, public LGBTQ narrative in both cases consequently offers a formidable chance to examine social change in each of the contexts more closely using Mill's concepts.

To provide empirical depth and an emic understanding of both cases, our research here relies on qualitative methods of study based on field research conducted in Tunisia during the summer 2014 and winter 2015 and in Lebanon during summer 2016 and winter 2017. During the fieldwork period, one of us conducted participant observation—including attendance of collective action, such as local protests—collecting interview data from local actors, including activists and artists. While most of the interviews were held in the capitals of Tunis and Beirut, the subjects were from across the country, providing for a mix between urban and rural participants (Noy 2008, 328–29). Additional key stakeholders involved in the transition process have also been interviewed when deemed appropriate, including policymakers, government experts, and practitioners. To select the research subjects, we used snowball sampling as a technique to reach out and tap into the network of different social groups that are hard to penetrate from outside. Oftentimes members of these groups form a closed-circle making it difficult for outsiders to gain access to the group and to obtain information (Noy 2008, 328–29). Snowball sampling therefore offers a way of collecting data by which the researcher uses the first point of contact of the social group under scrutiny, to get introduced to additional members within the network for further interviews and in-person meetings that serve to provide complementary data. Thus, with each additional member, the circle expands, allowing for a wide-cast net of participants who lie within the research study parameters. The objective of these interviews was to collect information about the varied involvements and trajectories of local actors at the time of the revolution and its aftermath, to capture different perceptions during the transition, and to compare a variety of views about conditions on the ground. Moreover, we employed content analysis to complement the data collected through research interviews. Documents include news articles retrieved from the written press and online sources, reports and official documents released by government institutions and non-governmental organizations, as well as information gathered from online blogs and social media such as Twitter and Facebook. These diverse sources were analyzed against the backdrop of discursive patterns indicating for instance countercultures or trends in public debates within Lebanese and Tunisian society and sub-cultures within different activist groups.

Mapping the Role of LGBTQ Activism in Tunisia and Lebanon

In the following, we map a variety of LGBTQ activism responses to the present conditions on the ground and explain to what extent these advocacy groups have created alternative spaces of deliberation in response to repressive politics and political injustices. We compare the Lebanese context to

Tunisian activists' efforts. This section focuses on a range of advocacy initiatives with alternative and artistic character traits. The objective is not to provide a holistic picture of each space of deliberation and the means employed to claim it[2]; but rather to provide an initial topography of the different forms of contestation and a critical evaluation of their purpose and impact.

The Role of Civil Society and the Power of Cyber Activism

The 2011 protests in Beirut did not spark the same wave of collective mobilization as the demonstrations caused by the death of Prime Minister Rafiq al-Hariri six years earlier. In 2005, during the so-called Cedar Revolution "some 1 million Christians, Muslims, and Druze from all parts of Lebanon gathered in Beirut, carrying signs and waving flags, to demonstrate for a free and independent Lebanon" (Jaafar and Stephan 2009, 169) The peaceful and nonviolent gatherings fueled a "critical juncture" for civil society to seize a political reform agenda (Clark and Zahar 2015, 2). However, civil society organizations did not seize the opportunity to reform Lebanese confession-based and consociational politics(Clark and Zahar 2015, 15). Lebanon's political context also translates into the current impasse and highly sectarian-influenced civil society that characterizes the space occupied by non-state actors.[3] The incremental rise of bottom-up movements, sparked by the 2005 Cedar Revolution and the recent "You stink" protests as a response to corrupt politics and governance issues failed to push for a reform agenda. Personality and interest-driven politics present challenging obstacles.

Under Ben Ali's regime, civil society in Tunisia was silenced a few years after he came to power in 1987, consolidating the strong state after an initial reform agenda (Alexander 1997, 34–38). While civil society started growing again in many Arab states, it was more due to authoritarian rulers' resilience strategies to remain in power (Cavatorta 2010, 25). The fall of Ben Ali changed the civil society landscape with "activists and projects mushrooming everywhere," underlines Nour Kaabi, a young activist who worked for the NGO Jamaity.[4] Many of these movements aimed at shifting societal beliefs and practices rather than institutional change (Jasper 1997, 70). This trend also holds true for LGBTQ activism, which was previously constrained to advocacy work focusing on public awareness of aids and sexual diseases.[5] Any advocacy work promoting a gay identity was unthinkable then. However, the revolution in Tunisia changed the situation on the ground for sexual minorities. They became visible, allowing them to advocate for equal rights, as a young activist, Sappho, recalls:

> Under Ben Ali, we had no visibility, but now homosexuality comes up in conversations and the media more often. Even if most of these comments are negative towards us at the moment, visibility is still a necessary first step towards equal rights.
>
> (cited in Rizvi 2014)

Since the revolution, several associations promoting LGBTQ rights have been created, such as Damj (Arabic for inclusion), which emphasizes the rights of sexual minorities (Fortier 2015, 9). Other organizations, including 'Without Restrictions' and Mawjoudin (Arabic for we exist), follow a similar strategy, due to the fear of legal repercussions if their mission statements were to openly support gay rights. Paragraph 230 of Tunisia's penal code prohibits consensual sex between two men, punishable by three years of prison. An exception is Shams (Arabic for sun), created in 2015, which openly fights for LGBTQ rights. However, hostile reactions from within Tunisian society and efforts by authorities to suspend their activities shortly after its creation posed serious challenges (Marzouk 2015a). Already in 2012, then Minister for Human Rights and Transitional Justice, Samir Dilou, denied the LGBTQ community the right to freely express themselves and stated that homosexuality was not a right but a perversion that required medical treatment (Dan Littauer 2012). In 2020, Shams won a legal victory handed down by Tunisia's Court of Cassation, defying the state's attempts to shut down the organization (al-Hilali 2020).

Claiming LGBTQ space in the Middle East remains challenging, as illustrated by the Lebanese gay community. In the early 2000s, the Queen Boat raid in Cairo led to the creation of Club Free, an underground LGBTQ social group accepting members only by invitation due to paranoia about police infiltration, explained Georges Azzi, former director of the club (cited in Benoist 2014a). The creation of Beirut-based NGO Helem in 2004 helped raise awareness of the LGBTQ community. However, internal tensions within Helem led to the creation of Meem, an independent women's group in 2007. Meem had a significant impact on raising awareness and educating society about LGBTQ issues. While physical presence was important, the internet served as a crucial platform for information dissemination.[6]

In Tunisia, many organizations have claimed cyberspace as their new battleground. Damj launched its Facebook page in 2013, fueling online activism that expands the Tunisian LGBTQ community. The founders of the first gay online magazine, *GayDay*, launched in 2011, were optimistic about expressing their lifestyle post-Ben Ali. However, hostile attitudes forced them to remain vigilant (*Deutsche Welle* 2012). Despite contested spaces, a cyberculture has developed, increasing visibility and recognition of LGBTQ members and youth activists, who are also victims of repressive politics due to increased extremism. Philip Howard defines cyberactivism as "using the Internet to advance a political cause that is difficult to advance offline ... [aiming to create] compelling digital artifacts that tell stories of injustice, interpret history, and advocate for particular political outcomes" (Howard 2011, 145).

An example is the Marwen case[7], a 22-year-old Tunisian man arrested for homosexual practices and subjected to an anal test. In 2015, he was sentenced to one year in prison. Several LGBTQ-friendly organizations, such as Shams, Mawjoudin and Damj, mobilized online campaigns with slogans including

"#FreeMarwen" and "Mawjoundin."[8] Although authorities refused Shams the permit for a public protest in support of Marwen's appeal, he received a reduced sentence and was released in January 2016.[9] Around the same time, the sentencing of six students from Kairouan on homosexuality charges garnered media attention in support of the LGBTQ cause (Marzouk 2015b).

Several LGBTQ organizations have been established since the revolution, with most not directly pointing to their LGBTQ cause in their mission statements to avoid being banned. This strategy allows the movement to operate more freely. The examples illustrate that "activists have not only integrated the Internet into their repertoire but also ... what counts as activism, what counts as community, collective identity, democratic space and political strategy" (McCaughey and Ayers 2003, 1–2). Mawjoudin organizes an annual queer film festival, requiring digital security and scrutiny to protect organizers and participants from threats and violence (Grace 2020).

The internet has played a crucial role in promoting a broader online culture regarding sexual orientation in Lebanon, opening a space for sexuality and desire. Since the 2005 protests, online platforms for the LGBTQ community have increased. "Through the vast global networks of queer websites, individuals in Lebanon have new opportunities for engaging with transnational currents of queer culture in the local context" (Gagné 2012, 124). The international queer movement, however, has been criticized by some as hegemonic interference with regional traditions and cultures (Massad 2007). The creation of a contested LGBTQ space in a fragmented society proves difficult and generates paradoxical outcomes, particularly regarding the body as a symbol of the power struggle for recognition.

GayRomeo.com, an international gay online dating platform available in Lebanon, requires users to create profiles based on an "aesthetic construction of the male body as hyper-masculine [which] reproduces normative standards of heterosexual masculinity" (Gagné 2012, 130). Despite GayRomeo. com's distinct objectives, it underscores the important role of identity formation processes and the associated politics. Introducing new categories to define alternative identities creates unease and challenges at various levels."But there is nothing easy about inhabiting new identities in what is inevitably and irreversibly a postcolonial, globalized modernity" (Mourad 2013, 2542). The internet has provided the LGBTQ community with tools to promote a new, alternative culture.

This culture remains contested in society. While virtual space has been claimed by youth since the revolution and freedom of expression has expanded, a political power struggle remains visible with territorial boundaries favoring the political elite. The marginalization of political Islam in Tunisia since the revolution, particularly in the media, has incited increasing dissident Islamist and Salafist voices online. While secularists have media access, religious dissidents have used the Internet as a counter-space to propagate their ideas (Branson 2014, 713–32).

Claiming Public Space through Street Art

The contested online space is complemented by a physical space, consisting of streets, walls and buildings. The message is still composed of words and images, but the medium is paint and spray cans. Street art and graffiti developed into one of the major forms of expression during and after the fall of the Ben Ali regime. In Lebanon, street art dates to the civil war period, when political factions used walls to spread their ideological discourse and foster identity politics across contested spaces (Chakhtoura 1978). Lebanese graffiti has evolved since, embracing aesthetics and politics. This section underlines several of these trends to explain the role of street art and youth in transitional contexts. By street art, the chapter refers to "the act of writing upon walls (also known as parietal writing) [which] is an equally ubiquitous and elemental act, one linked to the primal human desire to decorate, adorn, and physically shape the material environment" (Schacter and Fekner 2013, 9). But in the context of Tunisia and Lebanon, the significance of street art goes further. In fact, graffiti here represents a communication device that serves the purpose of transmitting a message from a collective group to the state (Chaffee 1993, 4). It has become a major weapon in the local and urban territorial disputes confronting the state and youth. When the waves of Tunisian protest descended over a large part of the country and the military and police forces lost control over the crowds, many protesters armed with spray cans and paint started claiming public spaces, marking slogans, symbols and images on walls, buildings and onto the street (Schriwer 2014, 376–91).

Many slogans that adorned walls and even street signs were painted in two languages: either in French and Arabic or in English and Arabic. The objective was to highlight the universal character of the publicly expressed messages. This was done against the backdrop of an internationalized transition with a corps of journalists invading the country to report on the unfolding of the events. Hence, their work was not only visible to the local eye, but to an international audience as well. A variety of messages were embedded in the art created across these urban spaces, including beautiful, detailed murals as well as crude, hastily sprayed anti-regime slogans on government buildings. The destruction of former regime property, such as one of the Ben Ali beach houses in Hammamet that was vandalized and covered in graffiti, attests to the angry appropriation of a space exclusively reserved for the ruling elites at the time.[10]

The post-war street art scene in Beirut, has shifted away from stenciled, political messages between groups involved in a perennial power struggle. Instead,

post-war graffiti ventured into issues of sexuality, equality, civic participation, and what I would generally characterise as new left campaigns militating, for example, for women's rights, lowering the voting age, gay rights, the reopening of the Beirut Forest to citizens, and especially against sectarianism.
(Kraidy 2016)

As a case in point, a young Beiruti street artist named Yazan Halwani paints large murals of revered Lebanese figures to alleviate sectarian tensions in a splintered city. He is writing "the stories of the city, on its own walls—creating a memory for the city" (cited in Bramley 2015). Bridging sectarian fault lines, he listens to members of the community and his depictions of prominent, historical personalities in his urban embellishment projects included figures, such as Samir Kassir, an assassinated Lebanese journalist and historian; Khalil Gibran, a feted Lebanese poet. In the summer of 2015, after over one year, he completed a project with Sabah, a famous Lebanese music diva in Beirut's buzzing Hamra district. The mural of the cultural icon, who passed away in 2014, a homage to Sabah's past glory, however, also delivers an important political message that goes beyond the singer's artistic fame. She also stands for a provocative counterculture in an often-conservative Arab world, with her multiple marriages and her scandalizing appearances. Yet, as Yazan Halwani underlines, "despite all the criticism against her and her response to it, she was still loved."[11] Her painted presence in the city's busy Hamra district therefore serves as a reminder that society requires spaces that contest the status quo and empower minority groups, such as the queer community and help fuel the existence of an alternative culture.

Gay activism has nonetheless seen waves of asserting increasing voices and visibility. For instance, the 2019 protests also known as "Thawra" (which translates to "uprising"), sparked by economic mismanagement and perennial sociopolitical malaise that overshadows the country, quickly turned into a platform for queer rights (Nagle 2023). While different sexual minorities, such as lesbian feminists, seized the opportunity to promote queer rights in the face of political marginalization and repression the advocacy strategies and activities embraced by these groups remain ambiguous. As John Nagle points out, "LGBTQ activism in the 2019 uprising lies a continuum of shades varying between direct and more concealed exposure" (Nagle 2023, 95).

In Tunisia, the LGBTQ movement has also seized this means of communication. Some of the graffiti dates to before the revolution, when members of the community used it as a form of subversive resistance to protest the witch hunt against homosexuals under Ben Ali's regime. One tag from 2008, for instance, shows an open padlock with a key, with the Arabic words asking when the penal code, particularly Article 230, will be "unlocked," i.e. reformed (see, for instance, Sbouai 2015). While the revolution fueled the community's high hopes for equal rights, the growing visibility in society also provoked violence and resentment against LGBTQ members and advocates. Myram, the co-founder of Chouf (Arabic for Look!), a feminist organization fighting for women's rights, deplores that "the violence has increased, you can feel it. Minorities in general have more and more been targeted. Being more visible has also made us more vulnerable. We've been victims of harassment and attacks since the revolution" (cited in Sbouai 2015, translated by the author). The wave of graffiti art since the revolution, however, has also inspired LGBTQ supporters to spread their message across public spaces. Tags and other street art have been particularly frequent in progressive parts of Tunisia's capital, Tunis, such as the La Marsa district, a liberal area with a high population of local artists and intellectuals. Slogans include messages such as "Love is not a crime" or "Stop Homophobia," often written in both Arabic and English or French. Yet, advocacy slogans to decriminalize sodomy in the country can also be seen next to the Tunisian Parliament in Le Bardo, an area reminiscent of Capitol Hill in Washington, DC.

Although the re-appropriation of space has long entered the political sphere through online campaigns and activism, the act of tagging physical spaces in the immediate proximity of the space where lawmakers decide on Tunisia's legislation creates a space in which the offline and online worlds collide. It provides activists with a new space to deliberate their views and ideas and confront decision-makers subversively. In addition, these ephemeral public forms of expression also engage non-queer communities in their everyday environment directly. This, of course, contrasts with the online spaces, which may be tailored for members of sexual minorities as the virtual areas are less visible than open, public spaces. Other art forms have followed suit since the revolution.

Performance Activism and Contentious Politics

In the visual and performing arts in Tunisia, the fall of Ben Ali fueled a spurt of creativity and an increase in artwork, illustrated by the growing number of art galleries in La Marsa.[12] Unsurprisingly the prospects of commodifying revolutionary art, in particular the idea of copying the tropes of the initial street art, inspired artists to sell their graffiti-inspired work on a globalized market (Howell 2013). Yet, such exposure did not result in art losing its sting, as some have argued elsewhere (Adams 2002, 21–56). Rather, in Tunisia's transitional context, this type of art played a vital role for the progressive and vanguard forces of the country. As Jacqueline Adams concisely put it in her work on women's protest under Pinochet in Chile, the women used it "for framing, to attract resources, to communicate information about themselves, to foster useful emotions, and as a symbol" (Adams 2002, 21–56). But in fragmented and fragile societies, these forms of expression and belonging can provoke tensions, as the following example illustrates. The ninth annual "Printemps des Art," an internationally renowned art exhibit in Tunis, turned into a clash of cultures and traditions in 2012, when a group of Salafists entered the premises and destroyed some of the art installations and threatened several artists, attacking the supposed blasphemous nature of the paintings, thus forcing the exhibit to shut down (Fordham 2012).[13]

In contrast to visual arts, music combines performative and discursive elements of political contestation in society. The case of Lebanese musicians' struggle to face not only conflict, but also fragile political institutions and social injustice, illustrates this phenomenon. Artists, including pianist Joelle

Khoury, oud player Ziyad Sahhab and death metal vocalist Garo Gdanian, were all born just before or at the beginning of the Lebanese civil war (1975–1990), and are all part of critical, musical voices in contemporary Lebanese society. Joelle Khoury, for instance, teaches at the Lebanese National Conservatory, and is actively engaged in non-commercial, non-programmatic music. While the war disrupted her education in her childhood and with it any chance to aspire to her professional music goals, 25 years after the end of the conflict the trauma still deeply affects society, as she described: "Here, everyone pretends to be happy, but everyone is still traumatized and very empty" (cited in Burkhalter 2011, 68). The hope originally sparked by the spillover effect of the Arab Spring did little to change the current situation. Neither did the Syrian conflict ravaging next door with thousands of refugees pouring into the country. Amid this chaos, however, the band Mashrou' Leila (Arabic for Night Project) with its lead vocalist Hamed Sinno, became a symbol of resilience, changing the tune of Lebanese politics. It is part of a rebellious surge of musical voices in the Middle East, including El Morabba3 and Zeid, which emerged around the time of the Arab spring, "creating a potent fusion of pop and politics" (Salfiti 2013). Yet Mr. Sinno is uncomfortable and skeptical about the symbolic role of his band as a pan-revolutionary platform for youth and protesters across the region. He explained that "To take one band and say these five people speak for all the disconnected political changes in an entire region, it's almost racist" (Fitch Little 2016). He criticizes any parallels with countries, such as Egypt, where thousands of people are in prison for raising their voices against the regime. Beirut is comparatively liberal. Mashrou' Leila's lyrics and music nonetheless hit a nerve in contemporary politics. As a gay frontman of the band, Mr. Sinno questions sexual stereotypes and redefines traditional identities of a new generation of young Lebanese with their songs resonating internationally.[14] Performances that serve as identity-enhancing acts by individuals or members or a social group are not a new phenomenon. "The dramatic unfolding of a queer presence in Beirut can often be ephemeral and finite in character, but it is one that asserts itself regularly" (Merabet 2014, 518). Spaces for members of the LGBTQ community have expanded, but constitute still veritable spaces of otherness, in which tolerance and acceptance oscillate between marginalization and violence.

The affirmation of these contested spaces, however, increasingly occurs in the visibility of open, public spaces. In connection with a growing religious conservatism in Tunisia due to the Ennahda-led government between 2011–2013, for instance, performance activism has also provoked a conservative outcry in Tunisian society. Amina Sboui, a women's rights activist, for instance, posted a topless picture of herself on Facebook during the March 2013 protests in honor of the assassinated Chokri Belaïd, an opposition leader. Her naked body contained the following message: "My body belongs to me and no one's source of honor" (M'Hiri 2013 text translated by the author). She was part of the feminist group FEMEN, a Paris-based organization that originated in Ukraine known for its topless protests and performance activism in public locations.[15] While it wasn't indecent exposure that caused her trouble with the law, she was eventually arrested later that spring in Kairouan, a conservative Bastion of the Salafist movement, while she tagged the word "FEMEN" on a wall near a Mosque (Dreisbach 2013). The juxtaposition of the virtual and physical space is further accentuated by the so-called Harlem Shake incident. In spring 2013, Tunisian students posted a comedy sketch with a song by US DJ Bauuer, causing the video to go viral inspiring memes in schools and universities around the country.[16] The secular youth's motives behind the dissemination of the message is summarized by Mohamed-Salah Omri as follows,

> Harlem shakers claim to represent life by setting their dancing and colourful costumes against a culture they see as preaching death and darkness – a reference to black niqabs and gowns worn by followers of Salafism, and their trademark black banner. Many Salafis, in turn, accuse the youth of being immoral and slavish imitators of "trashy" Western culture.
>
> (Omri 2013)

The Salafist movement's response to this form of public ridicule was prompt, retaliating with performances showcasing a strong political message. In fact, Salafi actions accentuated the instrumentalization of identity and belonging to contest this imaginary space as well as to protect and expand their own space. In addition to reinforcing symbols, such as black banners, niqabs, long shirts and skullcaps—practices that had increased under the troika government—members of the Salafi movement staged a couple of highly mediatized events. They stormed two public locations and captured one of the most representative symbols of the Tunisian state: the national flag on top of each of the occupied buildings. They then replaced them with the Salafist black banner on Manouba University campus and the clock tower on Bourguiba Avenue in the capital (Omri 2013). The boundaries between the imaginary and the real are thus intrinsically linked and the online space further fuels the contestation of the imagined spaces of each of the involved actors, including the state, secular as well as religious-oriented youth. The existing cleavages within society are therefore a political minefield putting conundrum in front of ruling elites, requiring them to elaborate an inclusive transition strategy to counterbalance increasing tensions, particularly with low acceptance rates of sexual minorities under ten percent ("Acceptance of Homosexuality in Tunisia 2013-2019," n.d.).

At present, Lebanese LGBTQ rights activists also face an uphill battle against preconceived images, particularly narratives of masculinity promoted by the state. While the "subversive activism" of the early 2000s has been "replaced by demobilized professionalization and NGOization," raids continue to shake the gay community (Benoist 2014b; Rizk and Makarem 2015).

Notwithstanding, the anti-LGBT discourse focuses on sexual behavior, but instead emphasizes the "performance of hetero- and homosexuality, specifically within a heteropatriarchal and capitalist system" (Benoist 2014b; Rizk and Makarem 2015) with paradoxical results. On the one hand, it enhances racial and class cleavages, as it pits a white, western ideal of homosexuality promoted by certain members of the LGBT community against poorer, marginalized individuals of Lebanon's gays. On the other hand, the constant local and regional security threats with the current war in Syria have forced organizations, such as Helem, to open their doors to a much larger group of individuals in need and provide them with a safe space, thus pushing internationalized and professionalized Helem staff to confront the heterogeneous reality of its community. Authorities at present, continue repression and raids against sexual minorities in the country (see, for instance, Younes 2023). Yet, as we will see in our following chapter, it is not necessarily the political instability and security threats that fuel repressive government action against LGBTQ communities. Sexual minorities in Singapore were targeted despite economic prosperity and the lack of state conflict.

Conclusion

Drawing on Foucault's concept of heterotopia, this study examined the role of LGBTQ activism and the use of art and collective action in post-Ben Ali Tunisia and contemporary Lebanon. The creation of new spaces for LGBTQ communities faces challenges from moral and security-based narratives. These spaces, both real and virtual, serve as sanctuaries and platforms for bottom-up advocacy, enabling communication and connection within the community. Despite increasing repression, social media and art have spearheaded a resilient movement. The Tunisian and Lebanese examples offer a model for neighboring regions, demonstrating how digital and artistic mediums can foster public debates on long-taboo subjects. This dynamic interplay between real and imaginary environments is crucial for understanding the struggles of LGBTQ communities in transitional societies.

Notes

1 The empirical findings for this chapter were first published as a chapter in Kurze (2020).
2 Between 2016 and 2018, the author is conducting a multidisciplinary project based on this initial research, including several institutional collaborators across the Maghreb.
3 Lebanese politics have been marked by a confession-based, consociational power-sharing structure since the nation's inception in 1943. Sectarian fault lines run deep and are reflected in the institutional setup. The presidency is reserved for a Christian Maronite, the post of the Prime Minister occupied by a member of the Sunni community and the seat of the Speaker of the House is left to a Shia parliamentarian.

4 Interviewed on 10 January 2015. The association is supported by international development agencies and donors including the United States, the European Union, Japan and the Arab Institute for Human Rights, among others.

5 For more details about their activities see http://www.atlmstsida.org/, accessed 20 April 2024.

6 See for instance Helem's website at http://www.helem.net/ and their Facebook page at https://www.facebook.com/Official-Page-for-Helem-Lebanon-133916233311662/, accessed 20 November 2016.

7 The pseudonym "Marwen" was given to the victim by activists in order to protect his identity.

8 See for instance https://www.facebook.com/hashtag/freemarwen?source=feed_text&story_id=606979069451821, accessed 3 January 2016.

9 See press release by Amnesty International, http://www.amnestyusa.org/get-involved/take-action-now/good-news-tunisia-marwan-released-ua-21615, accessed 15 January 2016.

10 The author visited the premises during his fieldwork in summer 2014.

11 See Yazan Halwani's YouTube video "Eternal Sabah," available at https://www.youtube.com/watch?v=MXAx85MtKtM, accessed 20 November 2016. Text translated by the author.

12 Interview with Laetitia Deloustal, art history scholar and researcher, on 17 January 2015.

13 See also an interview with Héla Ammar, artist and scholar, on 14 January 2015.

14 See Mashrou' Leila website at http://www.mashrouleila.com/, accessed 20 November 2016.

15 See FEMEN website at http://femen.org/, accessed 2 January 2015.

16 "Harlem Shake," originally a 1980s dance, refers to a song of the same name that became popular in 2012.

References

"Acceptance of Homosexuality in Tunisia 2013-2019." n.d. Statista. Accessed April 28, 2024. https://www.statista.com/statistics/1269974/acceptance-of-homosexuality-in-tunisia/.

Adams, Jacqueline. 2002. "Art in Social Movements: Shantytown Women's Protest in Pinochet's Chile." *Sociological Forum* 17 (1): 21–56.

Alexander, Christopher. 1997. "Back from the Democratic Brink: Authoritarianism and Civil Society in Tunisia." *Middle East Report*, 34–38.

Benoist, Chloé. 2014a. "Lebanese Gay Rights Organization Helem Marks 10 Years with a Mixed Legacy." *Al-Akhbar*, Sep, 30 2014. http://english.al-akhbar.com/node/21786.

Benoist, Chloé. 2014b. "Lebanese Security Forces Raid Gay-Friendly Establishment, Arrest 27." *Al-Akhbar*, August 13, 2014. http://english.al-akhbar.com/node/21131.

Bramley, Ellie Violet. 2015. "How a Beirut Graffiti Artist Is Using His Murals to Try to Unite a Fragmented City." *The Guardian*, September 22, 2015. http://www.theguardian.com/cities/2015/sep/22/beirut-graffiti-artist-yazan-halwani-lebanese.

Branson, Kayla. 2014. "Islamist Cyber-Activism: Contesting the Message, Redefining the Public." *The Journal of North African Studies* 19 (5): 713–32.

Burkhalter, Thomas. 2011. "Between Art for Art's Sake and Musical Protest: How Musicians from Beirut React to War and Violence." *Popular Music and Society* 34 (1): 55–77.

Cavatorta, Francesco. 2010. *Civil Society and Democratization in the Arab World: The Dynamics of Activism*. Abingdon: Routledge.

Chaffee, Lyman G. 1993. *Political Protest and Street Art: Popular Tools for Democratization in Hispanic Countries*. Westport: Greenwood Publishing Group.

Chakhtoura, Maria. 1978. *La Guerre Du Graffiti: Liban, 1975–1977*. Beyrouth: Dar An-Nahar.

Clark, Janine A., and Marie-Joëlle Zahar. 2015. "Critical Junctures and Missed Opportunities: The Case of Lebanon's Cedar Revolution." *Ethnopolitics* 14 (1): 1–18.

Dan Littauer, Pinknews. 2012. "Tunisian Human Rights Minister: No Free Speech for Gays." PinkNews. February 6, 2012. http://www.pinknews.co.uk/2012/02/06/tunisian-human-rights-minister-no-free-speech-for-gays/.

Deutsche Welle. 2012. "No Gay Rights Revolution in Tunisia," July 11, 2012. http://www.dw.com/en/no-gay-rights-revolution-in-tunisia/a-16364172.

Dreisbach, Tristan. 2013. "Femen Activist Amina Arrested Near Historic Mosque in Kairouan." *Tunisialive* (blog). May 21, 2013. http://www.tunisia-live.net/2013/05/20/femen-activist-amina-arrested-during-salafist-protests-in-kairouan/.

Fitch Little, Harriet. 2016. "Hamed Sinno, Frontman of the Arab World's Hottest Indie Band." *Financial Times*, October 7, 2016. https://www.ft.com/content/34df8710-8a87-11e6-8cb7-e7ada1d123b1.

Fordham, Alice. 2012. "L'Art Face à l'Intégrisme." *Courrier International*, June 28, 2012. http://www.courrierinternational.com/article/2012/06/28/l-art-face-a-l-integrisme

Fortier, Edwige A. 2015. "Transition and Marginalization: Locating Spaces for Discursive Contestation in Post-Revolution Tunisia." *Mediterranean Politics*, 20(2): 1–19.

Gagné, Mathew. 2012. "Queer Beirut Online." *Journal of Middle East Women's Studies* 8 (3). http://www.academia.edu/download/30571396/Gagne_Queer_Beirut_online_The_participation_of_men_in_Gayromeo.com.pdf

Grace, Ryan. 2020. "Digital Security and the LGBTI+ Rights Movement in Tunisia." Middle East Institute. April 22, 2020. https://www.mei.edu/publications/digital-security-and-lgbti-rights-movement-tunisia.

Hilali, Amel al-. 2020. "LGBTQ Association Achieves Major Legal Milestone in Tunisia." Al-Monitor: Independent, Trusted Coverage of the Middle East. March 5. https://www.al-monitor.com/originals/2020/03/tunisia-shams-association-gay-rights-legal-presence.html

Howard, Philip N. 2011. *The Digital Origins of Dictatorship and Democracy Information Technology and Political Islam*. Oxford: Oxford University Press.

Howell. 2013. "Graffiti Inspires Tunisia Artists." Online. *BBC NEWS Africa*. BBC. http://www.bbc.co.uk/news/world-africa-21401434

Jaafar, Rudy, and Maria Stephan. 2009. "Civilian Jihad: Nonviolent Struggle, Democratization, and Governance in the Middle East." In *Civilian Jihad: Nonviolent Struggle, Democratization, and Governance in the Middle East*, edited by Maria Stephan, 2009 edition, 169–85. London: Palgrave Macmillan.

Jasper, James M. 1997. *The Art of Moral Protest: Culture, Biography, and Creativity in Social Movements*. Chicago: University of Chicago Press.

Kraidy, M. M. 2016. *The Naked Blogger of Cairo*. Cambridge: Harvard University Press.

Kurze, Arnaud. 2020. "Seeking New Metaphors: Gender Identities in Tunisia and Lebanon." In *Arab Spring: Modernity, Identity and Change*, edited by Eid Mohamed and Dalia Fahmy, 207–33. Cham: Springer International Publishing.

Lijphart, Arend. 1975. "II. The Comparable-Cases Strategy in Comparative Research." *Comparative Political Studies* 8 (2): 158–77.

Marzouk, Zeineb. 2015a. "Gay Rights Group Fights for the Right to Exist." *Tunisialive*, December 3, 2015. http://www.tunisia-live.net/2015/12/03/gay-rights-group-fights-for-the-right-to-exist/

Marzouk, Zeineb. 2015b. "Kairouan: Six Examined, Imprisoned and Banished on Charges of Homosexuality." *Tunisialive*, December 14, 2015. http://www.tunisia-live.net/new/2015/12/14/kairouan-six-examined-imprisoned-and-banished-on-charges-of-homosexuality/

Massad, Joseph. 2007. *Desiring Arabs*. Chicago, IL: University of Chicago Press.

McCaughey, Martha, and Michael D. Ayers. 2003. *Cyberactivism: Online Activism in Theory and Practice*. Abingdon: Routledge.

Merabet, Sofian. 2014. "Queer Habitus: Bodily Performance and Queer Ethnography in Lebanon." *Identities* 21 (5): 516–31.

M'Hiri, Yüsra. 2013. "'Mon Corps M'appartient et Il N'est L'honneur de Personne.'" *Courrier International*, March 20, 2013. http://www.courrierinternational.com/article/2013/03/20/mon-corps-m-appartient-et-il-n-est-l-honneur-de-personne.

Mourad, Sara. 2013. "Doing It| Queering the Mother Tongue." *International Journal of Communication Systems* 7:14.

Nagle, John. 2023. "Somewhere over the Rainbow: The Symbolic Politics of In/visibility in Lebanese Queer Activism." In *Symbolic Objects in Contentious Politics*, 80–100. Ann Arbor: University of Michigan Press.

Noy, Chaim. 2008. "Sampling Knowledge: The Hermeneutics of Snowball Sampling in Qualitative Research." *International Journal of Social Research Methodology* 11 (4): 327–44.

Omri, Mohamed-Salah. 2013. "Tunisia Tries to Stop the Harlem Shake." *The Guardian*, March 7, 2013. http://www.theguardian.com/world/2013/mar/07/tunisia-harlem-shake

Rizk, A., and G. Makarem. 2015. "'Masculinity-under-Threat': Sexual Rights Organizations and the Masculinist State in Lebanon." *Civil Society Review*. http://civilsociety-centre.org/sites/default/files/papers/risk-makarem_en.pdf

Rizvi, Aman. 2014. "Homosexuals in Tunisia: Still in the Shadows." *TunisiaLive*, July 16. http://www.tunisia-live.net/2014/07/16/homosexuals-in-tunisia-still-in-the-shadows/.

Salfiti, Jad. 2013. "Mashrou' Leila: The Lebanese Band Changing the Tune of Arab Politics." *The Guardian*, September 13, 2013. http://www.theguardian.com/music/musicblog/2013/sep/13/mashrou-leila-lebanese-arab-politics

Sbouai, Sana. 2015. "Homosexualité: La Bataille Au Grand Jour." *Inkyfada*, May 17. https://inkyfada.com/2015/05/homosexualite-bataille-au-grand-jour-tunisie/

Schacter, Rafael, and John Fekner. 2013. *The World Atlas of Street Art and Graffiti*. New Haven: Yale University Press.

Schriwer, Charlotte. 2014. "Graffiti Arts and the Arab Spring." In *Routledge Handbook of the Arab Spring: Rethinking Democratization*, edited by Larbi Sadiki, 376–91. Abingndon : Routledge.

Younes, Rasha. 2023. "Lebanon: Attack on Freedoms Targets LGBTI People." Human Rights Watch. September 5, 2023. https://www.hrw.org/news/2023/09/05/lebanon-attack-freedoms-targets-lgbti-people

5 Neocolonial Legacies and Queerness in Singapore

Over the past few decades, Singapore's explosive growth from a small colonial outpost into a global trading hub has been considered by many as a modern socioeconomic miracle. Against all odds, the state has managed to leverage the benefits of rapid modernization to emerge as a multicultural haven, where adherence to the rule of law has become its defining feature. However, one persistent criticism of the country, and by extension, the long-ruling People's Action Party (PAP), has been its paternalistic approach to individual civil liberties. This is especially true for the LGBTQ community, which has long experienced discrimination and relegation as second-class citizens. In this regard, the ruling elite has followed the "Asian values" ideology as promoted by long-serving Prime Minister Lee Kuan Yew. This sociopolitical framework "argued that individual political rights were unnecessary luxuries that should come after the rights of the community, the economy, and the state" (Ciocchini and Radics 2019, 33). Hence, the outlook that has guided the country to its economic successes has also significantly influenced how society interprets behaviors and concepts that are deemed foreign, with non-heteronormative identities being depicted as "non-Singaporean."

A common thread amidst this intersection of queer rights and citizenship has been the legacy of colonial rule. Singapore is one of many ex-colonies that are still grappling with the effects of British-era penal codes. Laws such as Section 377A—which criminalized sex between consenting adult males—have led to enduring linkages between homosexuality and immorality. Though these codes have been repealed—albeit very recently in 2023 for Singapore—the societal effects of these laws in combination with a conservative state apparatus have created a dynamic environment in which sexual minorities are forced to consider pragmatic priorities alongside their desire for greater equality.

Local queer rights activists have demonstrated a remarkable ability to navigate between the state's hegemonic control and conservative social forces. Non-confrontational strategies of advocacy are commonplace, chosen to avoid perceptions of threatening a delicate status quo. Activism that works alongside and within the state's system is mostly preferred in contrast to

DOI: 10.4324/9781003565871-8

more confrontational modes of direct protest. The latter also risks being negatively depicted as a "Western" approach to conflict resolution. As academic Lynette J. Chua notes, "engaging transnational movements, and deploying international human rights discourse can attract accusations of abandoning one's indigenous culture, and proselytizing Western influences" (Chua 2012, 721). Hence, multiple dilemmas and pathways exist when determining the best course of action for LGBTQ advocacy, especially since it must factor in complex linkages with broader disputes over identity, nationhood, and sovereignty. While non-confrontational tactics have resulted in gradual progress, it remains to be seen how this momentum can be sustained if change remains a top-down process, in a state that values pragmatism and social stability above all else.

Colonial Rule, Homophobia, and the Impact on Sexual Minorities

The positioning of LGBTQ rights amidst debates on identity and postcolonial politics can be better understood through tracing how homophobic norms became embedded during foreign imperial rule. Such developments have not been unique to Singapore nor to the Southeast Asian region. In Namibia, the modern-day rise of "politicized homophobia" can be traced back to colonial anti-sodomy laws. Political elites now use these laws to shore up popular support, ironically portraying "same-sex sex as an unwanted colonial import… [and] (LGBT) rights as continuing Western imperialism." For Singapore, the Straits Settlement Penal Code of 1871 provides a similar starting point. It was virtually identical to the Indian Penal Code enacted in 1860, underscoring its significance for legislative standardization across Britain's colonies. Human Rights Watch notes, the "Indian Penal Code, [was] the first experiment in producing a criminal code anywhere in the Empire" (Watch 2013, 91). The legislation was a means for the colonizing power to deepen its control over all strata of society. Matters related to sexuality were interpreted through Anglo-Christian notions of propriety and morality, reflecting contemporary anxieties regarding racial purity. This was evident in the "urgency British authorities showed in transplanting 'sodomy' laws into colonial contexts" (Watch 2013, 92), as such acts became correlated with the "fears of moral infection from the 'native' environment[s]" (Watch 2013, 94). Protecting colonial interests involved segregating and reforming "civilized" and "native" features, in the colonizer's image. The Indian Penal Code was drafted with two notable distinctions regarding sodomy: a recurring "traditional discomfort" when outlining acts that violated "the order of nature" (Watch 2013, 94), and uncertainty over whether consent should alter how these acts were punished. This complexity arose from societal norms that saw open discussion about these issues as distasteful, with administrators working "under the shadow of a moral anxiety about the effects of debate" (Watch 2013, 100). These influential legal frameworks were not fully developed through adequate deliberation, nor did they consider local customs in matters of morality or private behavior.

Punishing Sexual Practices in Singapore's Early Years of Independence

In resolving these ambiguities, consent was suggested as a variable, with non-consensual acts of sodomy warranting harsher punishment (Watch 2013, 94). When this clause was ultimately dropped, meant homosexual acts were lumped together with crimes like same-sex rape or pedophilia, leading to victims facing the same charges as perpetrators. The legislation created enduring linkages between homosexuality and criminal behavior, highlighting political control potential (Watch 2013, 95). These tensions laid the groundwork for further marginalization of non-heteronormative citizens as Singapore transitioned from a colony to an independent state. The nation's early years were marred by sociopolitical and economic challenges, influencing the emergence of a one-party system under Prime Minister Lee Kuan Yew and the People's Action Party (PAP). George Radics notes that "in 1965, it was a tiny city-state expelled from its larger neighbor, reliant on a few staples of production with an inconsiderable local market and a swelling immigrant population" (Ciocchini and Radics 2019, 35). The fledgling state lacked a powerful shared history, with most inhabitants identifying with the "cultural homeland[s] of their ethnic group," and independence, gained without revolution, preventing unity through shared sacrifice (Tan 2015, 973). The population's heterogeneity across racial and religious divides, created constant fears of inter-ethnic violence. Economic prosperity was endorsed as a solution to ensure civic unity, promoting pragmatism and meritocracy as the determinants of worth in society (Ciocchini and Radics 2019, 35). This exacerbated postcolonial tensions, linking queer rights with foreignness and societal corruption.

Sexual Minorities Navigating the Treacherous Legal Spaces in Daily Life

In this restricted environment, sexual rights remained secondary until the 1980s, when the government became "concerned that Singaporean values were becoming wayward due to the influx of wealth and new vices" (Ciocchini and Radics 2019, 35). The state intervention that created prosperity would now guide private lives and personal character. This structural design, along with societal tensions, illustrates the complex issue of cultural and sexual citizenship in Singapore. Those who do not conform to the heteronormative standard are handicapped as a byproduct of a nation-building strategy that relies on stability, pragmatism, and rapid economic development. To design a productive society and appease its conservative minorities, aspects of national belonging were selectively defined. Homeownership was one battleground—societal hierarchies determined access to public housing units, requiring a minimum age of 21, and a "state-defined proper family nucleus" (Tan 2015, 974). Given that gay marriage was and remains illegal, homosexual couples were ineligible, resigning them to wait until the age of 35 for public housing or settle for costlier alternatives on the resale market (Tan 2015, 974). As Chris Tan notes, "queers are welcomed for their economic productivity, but their refusal to partake in reproductive marital life renders them partial citizens" (Tan 2015, 977). Law enforcement also harassed queer citizens, monitoring known meeting spots, and engaging in "entrapment" where they posed as gay men in order to "promptly arrest anyone who engaged with them" (Wong 2022).

Civilian attempts to address these injustices were difficult due to constraints under the PAP rule. Protests were nearly non-existent, since "forming of associations of 10 or more persons is illegal without state approval" (Chua 2012, 716). Media censorship banned content justifying or glamorizing "lifestyles such as homosexuality, lesbianism, bisexualism, transsexualism [and] transvestism" (Chua 2012, 716). These restrictions gradually relaxed from the 2000s as PAP leadership allowed limited debate, with the rise of Internet access creating virtual spaces where censorship was comparatively laxer.

State Conservatism: Understanding the Link Between Instability and Repressive Practices

To better understand why the state continues to uphold this delicate status quo, it is vital to understand why this top-down system is seen as the best solution for societal stability. Unresolved fears of communal unrest have potently combined with longstanding norms linking homosexuality with criminal behavior and immorality, explaining the common refrains that repeatedly emerge on the rare occasions when queer issues are publicly debated. During the 2007 parliamentary review of the Penal Code, supporters of Section 377A "trumpeted 'family values' and 'majority morality,' and warned against the grand 'homosexual agenda.'" (Chen 2013, 107–8) In opposition, those who advocated for repealing 377A "rallied for 'liberty' and 'equality,'" emphasizing the right to privacy as well as highlighting the foreign origins of the Penal Code. In this instance, the government chose to maintain 377A and reiterate its commitment towards traditional values, but also sought to appease both sides by noting that 377A "would not be proactively enforced against consensual private acts not involving minors" (cited in Chen 2013, 107–8).

Yet we also ought to turn to more recent developments, which illustrate how civilian-led initiatives have influenced state behavior, legal reforms, and public attitudes concerning queer rights. Section 377A, firmly entrenched since the colonial era, was finally repealed in January 2023. This watershed moment can be attributed to the tireless advocacy efforts by local activists and grassroots organizers, whose work has had to contend with the mixture of colonial-era prejudices, state-led marginalization, as well as societal stigmatization. Nonetheless, the repeal still featured familiar elements previously seen in 2007, with the state attempting to maintain its image of neutrality by reaffirming its commitment to marriage as being between man and woman ("Constitution of the Republic of Singapore (Amendment No. 3) Act 2022 - Singapore Statutes Online," n.d.). In voicing their disapproval of the repeal, several Members of Parliament once again touched upon "family values," faith-based arguments, as well as a "fear of being cancelled" for conservative citizens who may wish to voice their concerns about homosexuality (Min 2022). Majority-minority politics between conservative and progressive voices therefore continue to be a main point of contention, where queer rights are framed as a disruptive movement that threatens to undermine the hard-won social harmony and stability that was so carefully managed since the country's inception.

Queer Activism in Singapore: Stories from the Trenches[1]

Given this context, queer activism is almost by nature required to operate in a highly dynamic manner, adapting to shifting legal and societal opinions while also effectively meeting the needs of a long-marginalized community. Understanding the strategies and decisions involved therefore required a direct connection with local stakeholders. To achieve this, the authors conducted interviews with several Singaporean LGBTQ activists to capture their views on non-confrontational activism, as well as how they viewed their work in the context of the restrictions present in Singapore. To ensure a level of diversity, their experience varied from localized outreach work to large nationwide events. Combined with existing academic literature, the data from these interviews provide us with important insights on recurring themes that exist within Singapore's LGBTQ activism space.

Catering to Preconceived Heteronormative Values in Society

Interviewee, "Chris,"[2] utilized his background in photography and film to spread awareness on the various legal and societal issues that queer families faced. Some of these themes were communicated via an art collective that hosted public exhibits. In describing the challenges of planning such events, he noted the recurring tendency towards self-censorship. Since public event applications were subject to review by government agencies, LGBTQ-themed topics are particularly vulnerable to age-related restrictions on attendance. In our conversation with Chris, he shared his experience about filing for a permit. The application process included a discussion on whether terms like "LGBTQ" should even be included when describing their intended programming, or whether subtler euphemisms could get around censors. When it was agreed that such workarounds would probably not fool the censor board, the art collective decided to view this as an opportunity to make the most of the age-restricted rating and "push the bracket," exhibiting pieces that showed everyday displays of affection between queer couples like kissing. However, Chris noted that "it does ache," in reference to the disappointment in having to turn away teenage attendees, especially given their importance and heightened vulnerability as a demographic. Ultimately, he stressed the challenges that came with engaging broader audiences. The desire to ensure an inclusive and relatable discourse made it feel necessary to present LGBTQ issues in a way that was in line with broader, mainstream sensibilities, prioritizing event permit approval over addressing more specific concerns.

Similar experiences with navigating self-censorship were also mentioned by another interviewee, "Jessica." As a transgender activist who worked to provide housing and counseling services for at-risk transgender individuals, Jessica underlined that LGBTQ advocacy work often involves knowing how to make certain issues more palatable for a heteronormative and less receptive society. This reflected the prevailing standards that constrain options for activism—in a study on these matters, Robert Phillips noted that the success of events like the Pink Dot parade was due to the organizers' explicit declaration that it was not a protest, as well as ensuring that it would not be "overtly sexual" (Phillips 2014, 50–1). In Jessica's experience, these considerations were especially true when it came to pursuing public funding and other governmental interactions such as registering her organization. She stated, "At the time, I wanted to get registered as a legal entity. I was rejected twice, because at that time, anything 'LGBT' could not be registered. In my company profile I [had] put 'shelter for transgender women.'" When someone suggested removing LGBTQ-related words from the company profile, Jessica refused, stating that it felt like she was erasing her own identity. This issue was eventually resolved when she attended a workshop where a high-ranking minister was present, allowing her a chance to inform him personally of the struggles in getting registered. Interestingly, the application was eventually approved a few months after this meeting.

The Importance of Strategic Framing of LGBTQ Issues

When asked about how she navigated these situations, Jessica noted the importance of framing advocacy work in a manner that appealed to state interests. The concept of "helping hands" was brought up—a term which reflects the government's desire for the population to act collectively in upholding social stability, rather than engaging in individualistic behavior that risked disorder. Hence, she attributes her success in part to being aware of these dynamics and tactfully emphasizing her work in a pragmatic lens, framing it as addressing common-ground issues like homelessness without necessarily obscuring its dedicated focus on the transgender community. In this respect, Jessica also explained how approaches rooted in universal rights language, as exemplified by her distaste for generic terms like "empowerment," often fell short in addressing local needs. First, it diverts attention away from practical realities—in this case, the issue of homelessness among the transgender population—since idealistic phrasing can become unintentionally confrontational by virtue of being abstract and subjective. Second, such approaches fail to account for the state's far-reaching authority. By not appealing to the state's clear preference for pragmatism and stability, idealistic approaches can easily fall victim to appearing impractical at best or socially subversive at worst, both of which limit the extent to which these projects can operate freely or obtain public funding. Thus, as Jessica states, the framing of her work is paramount in maintaining its ability to be effective within the existing system. Even her secondary project—a community center offering counseling and social services for the transgender community—is carefully marketed as a youth mental health resource depending on the audience. Nonetheless, Jessica clearly states that she doesn't overlook the importance of empowering her community, but rather that such ideals are more achievable via low-key, pragmatic actions within an environment like Singapore.

In addition to accounting for the sensibilities of a conservative general audience, external influences are also another key determinant of how activism will be perceived. "Rachel," another interviewee, is a founder of an online organization that provides guidance and resources for family and friends of queer individuals. Initially, their new group was modeled after PFLAG (Parents, Families and Friends of Lesbians and Gays), which is the United States' largest organization "dedicated to supporting, educating, and advocating for LGBTQ+ people and those who love them" ("About Us" 2022). Although PFLAG provided a relevant model for the work that Rachel wanted to accomplish, she was careful not to emphasize this influence too publicly. She stated, "we [didn't] want to use the same name because it has its own baggage, and people will think it has all the Western influences." This cognizance further reflects the importance of a homegrown approach, as it shields activists from accusations of ulterior motives or undue influence, both of which are common refrains in portraying homosexuality as an unwelcome foreign import.

Coping with Social Context: Stereotypes, Bias, and Prejudice

Understanding how to navigate societal prejudices and stereotyping of homosexuality was a key focus for another interviewee, "Ryan." A gay man who has worked in LGBTQ advocacy for over a decade, Ryan was also one of the founders of a large nationwide queer rights movement. What made this organization unique was its ability to coordinate large-scale gatherings, where queer individuals and straight allies could display their support for greater equality. Much like Jessica's strategic presentation of her work, Ryan noted that his organization had to be extremely mindful of potential backlash, requiring their activities to prioritize broad palatability and avoid alienating the public. At the time, this meant emphasizing the fact that "this was not a protest, it's more a celebration of love," with marketing materials that were "very much an appeal to straight allies, not necessarily directly to the [queer] community." Given that public gatherings were still a novel concept due to tight censorship, Ryan's approach allowed for both participants and observers to avoid the heightened tensions that would be associated with direct confrontation, and instead reiterate the queer community's right to integrate as equals within Singaporean society. While it was a major success and turned into an annual event, there were considerable challenges in representing the diverse non-heteronormative community. Ryan was reflective on the shortcomings of his organization's early years. The preoccupation with ensuring palatability and broad support had the unintended consequences of overlooking how certain subgroups experienced different levels of marginalization and stigma. He noted that the original event's "whole emphasis [was] on love and not sex, [and] we may have taken that a little too far." He recalled that they had declined to allow the participation of a sex workers' rights organization over concerns that it could "make the event less family friendly." By subsequently highlighting how many sex workers in Singapore are transgender, Ryan illustrated how these two criticisms required the organization to grow to avoid intra-communal biases, incorporating changes such as ensuring greater diversity in its leadership committee to avoid overrepresentation of the "Chinese cis gay man."

Organic Linkages between LGBTQ Identities and Community Structures

Asides from strategic presentation of activism work, another common theme was the extent in which the interviewees self-identified as activists. All four interviewees did not set out with clear intentions on being advocates; rather, their work grew out of a natural desire to give back to their community. Chris' experience began as he wanted to utilize his art media background for subject matters that were deeply personal to him. Yet, after several years of involvement in such work, he still hesitates to identify himself and his art collective as full-fledged activists. Rather, he describes himself and his work as being "passion projects... vehicles to push for acceptance."

For Jessica, her journey was a progression from her time as a sex worker, after which she became involved in public speaking on transgender issues. The shelter then grew out of an earlier project where the focus was initially on foreign domestic workers, with Jessica using a similar concept to help address housing issues within the transgender community. During this early stage of her career, she describes her confusion over whether her work qualified her as an activist. "At that time, my image of activism was that I had to fight for rights, [that I] must go against the government, and then I would be jailed for my activism... but then they said 'No, a shelter is also human rights.'" Building upon this realization, Jessica stated that she began rethinking activism as a concept, noting that popular Western-centric rhetoric often sidelined practical issues in favor of abstracted universal rights claims. Given her decision to remain firmly dedicated toward these tangible everyday issues, Jessica stated that "I don't see myself as an activist. I see myself as an employee... the only thing I want to grow is the impact for my community." From her perspective, local understandings of activism also carry connotations of elitism, where "in Singapore, all the activists are all elite. All are university students, most probably have PhDs, lived overseas, have their own flats or landed properties."

As Robert Phillips argues, the appearance of conformity and tactical alignment with the status quo can be termed as "illiberal pragmatics," where concerns about survival intermingle with a deeper desire for full acceptance and citizenship (Phillips 2014, 48). Phillips emphasizes this point through the example of Otto Fong, a 38-year-old science teacher who blogged about his journey as a homosexual man in 2007 amidst the ongoing parliamentary review over Section 377A. Fong described himself as "a son, a brother, a long-time companion, an uncle, a teacher, a classmate, a colleague, a part of your community, a HDB dweller, a Singaporean," before concluding his post with the highly significant sentence, "And I am also gay" (Phillips 2014, 45–6). Thus, Jessica's hesitancy in self-identifying as an activist is indicative of this continued struggle. If integration and equality alongside the status quo is the end goal, local structures have made it so that this can only be achieved through demonstrating that one is not a threat to the heteronormative mainstream. In this respect, a gay identity in Singapore is incentivized to not "challenge the 'dominant heteronormative assumptions and institutions but upholds and sustains them'" (Phillips 2014, 46). It is this ability to support the status quo and assimilate alongside other Singaporeans who share this national identity that can therefore demonstrate that queer individuals are equally capable of being "good Singaporeans." Queer advocates are therefore challenged to create progress despite overt activism being closely linked with undesirable individualism and foreign values—their advocacy, if conducted without careful consideration, is easily turned into a demonstration of their unsuitability as Singaporeans.

As societal acceptance increases alongside growing visibility for the queer community, counter-movements have also been increasingly extreme and vocal. With the government holding fast to its moderating role between conservative and progressive forces, this has also created new dilemmas on how LGBTQ rights movements can respond to spoilers. Our interviewee Rachel described the actions of conservative opposition forces as "Trumpian," due to the use of a "post-truth, alternate facts" approach. As a result of these strategies, it creates an issue on how to deal with "bad faith actors," where further engagement likely only results in deepening animosity between groups. This presents a clear challenge for local activists, and it remains to be seen whether non-confrontational tactics can overcome such contention.

Conclusion

The prevailing postcolonial atmosphere, alongside Singapore's uniquely pragmatic approach to sociopolitical affairs, has created an intensely complex environment within which the queer community is forced to reckon with uncertainty over their marginalized roles. The prejudices that influenced British-era legislation have survived beyond decolonization, making its mark on modernity through a subtler weaponization of the law against sexual minorities. For these communities, acting against these injustices risks further ostracization, or turning counterproductive if outspoken activism is portrayed as unbefitting to the collective identity that underpins Singapore's national identity. In turn, the interviewees' self-identification and self-perception on their own work goes to show that concepts like "activism" is highly subjective, as well as highly contextual to the location and culture in which it is practiced. In a tightly controlled state, the government itself plays a significant role in influencing how such terms are interpreted by its population, as well as the implicit connotations these terms carry. When combined with the perception that certain modes of advocacy may be too "Western," it begins to explain certain contradictions that are apparent. People may engage in actions that clearly fall under a general definition of advocacy work but may hesitate to see or label it as such. This appears to be influenced by the necessity to operate tangentially to the state's interests, disincentivizing any overt dissent or confrontation.

Additionally, the societal reverence for pragmatic and practical values further encourages advocates to frame their work as an extension of their desire to help, rather than verbalizing it through the abstract idealism of universal rights language. This is not to say that more confrontational or radical approaches are non-existent; all four interviewees noted existing intra-communal tensions where some LGBTQ activists are eager for greater progress, while others prefer to maintain the tried-and-true approaches. Instead, observers must understand that such strategies are already highly adapted to the local context. Rather than judging advocacy groups for shying away from confronting the status quo or for aligning with the state's hegemonic role, more attention is needed on the extent to which such groups and individuals can enact positive change on the local level. Thus, this allows a better understanding of how universal human rights values are protected under more restrictive environments and asks whether such conditions incentivize more holistic approaches toward advocacy.

As seen in the following chapter and its examination of illiberalism in Poland, Singapore is far from unique in how queer rights have become enmeshed within broader debates on national identity, sovereignty, and international integration. Rapidly shifting social landscapes have increased the value of mass political mobilization, which in turn caters to actors that are able to utilize inflammatory rhetoric and heavily simplify complex issues at play. To combat the promotion of LGBTQ persons as a scapegoat for national decay, activists have reframed transnational strategies of protest to suit their local contexts, allowing them to recapture narratives from spoiler groups that have portrayed queer rights as a foreign subversive threat.

Notes

1 These interviews were conducted between September 2023 to January 2024.
2 We have used separate identifiers to protect the privacy of our participants given the repressive environment in Singapore.

References

"About Us." 2022. PFLAG. PFLAG National. November 23, 2022. https://pflag.org/about-us/.

Chen, Jianlin. 2013. "Singapore's Culture War over Section 377A: Through the Lens of Public Choice and Multilingual Research: Singapore's Culture War over Section 377A." *Law & Social Inquiry: Journal of the American Bar Foundation* 38 (01): 106–37.

Chua, Lynette J. 2012. "Pragmatic Resistance, Law, and Social Movements in Authoritarian States: The Case of Gay Collective Action in Singapore: Pragmatic Resistance." *Law & Society Review* 46 (4): 713–48.

Ciocchini, Pablo, and George Radics. 2019. *Criminal Legalities in the Global South: Cultural Dynamics, Political Tensions, and Institutional Practices*. Abingdon: Routledge.

"Constitution of the Republic of Singapore (Amendment No. 3) Act 2022 - Singapore Statutes Online." n.d. Accessed 29 July, 2024. https://sso.agc.gov.sg:5443/Acts-Supp/40-2022/Published/20230103?DocDate=20230103.

Min, Ang Hwee. 2022. "Faith, Conscience and a Future without 377A: What MPs Said While Debating Laws on Gay Sex and Marriage." CNA. November 30, 2022. https://www.channelnewsasia.com/singapore/mps-377a-marriage-gay-sex-constitution-religion-3111901.

Phillips, R. 2014. "And I Am Also Gay": Illiberal Pragmatics, Neoliberal Homonormativity and LGBT Activism in Singapore. *Anthropologica* 56 (1): 45–54.

Tan, Chris K. K. 2015. "Pink Dot: Cultural and Sexual Citizenship in Gay Singapore." *Anthropological Quarterly* 88 (4): 969–96.

Watch, Human Right. 2013. "This Alien Legacy: The Origins of 'sodomy'laws in British Colonialism." Human Rights, Sexual Orientation and Gender Identity in The Commonwealth, 83–124.

Wong, Tessa. 2022. "377A Repeal: Singapore Turns Page on Dark LGBT History." *BBC News*, December 4, 2022. https://www.bbc.co.uk/news/world-asia-63832825.

6 Religion, Illiberalism, and Queer Struggles in Poland

The interplay between religion, illiberalism, and queer struggles in Poland offers a compelling lens through which to explore the development of queer activism in a context marked by cultural and political resistance. This chapter delves into the unique trajectory of LGBTQ activism in Poland, tracing its evolution from the post-communist transformation era to the contemporary challenges faced by the community. The fall of communism in Poland ushered in significant social and political changes, many of which were shaped by the country's integration into the European Union in 2004. Despite this integration, Poland's journey has been fraught with cultural-religious opposition and democratic crises that have distinctly influenced the modalities of LGBTQ activism compared to other Central and Eastern European states and EU members.

Central to the discussion is the notion of gender ideology, a term weaponized by Polish right-wing factions to oppose various gender and sexual equality initiatives. Initially used by right-wing campaigns opposing the teaching of sex education in Polish schools and the ratification of the Istanbul Convention, its adherents grew to include anyone opposed to abortion access and any initiatives whose proponents supposedly intended "to dismantle the 'traditional' family, the nation, and ultimately, 'Christian civilisation'" (Korolczuk 2020, 166). Since the spring of 2019, however, due to opposition on popular and legal fronts, particularly on the issue of judicial overreach in the name of abortion restrictions, "the main enemy of ultraconservative forces has been LGBT people" (Korolczuk 2020, 166), and the struggle against gender ideology has increasingly given way to a campaign against LGBT ideology. In a similar fashion to American anti-gay rights campaigns of the 1970s, "Polish anti-gender activists spread false information suggesting that gay men are disproportionally more prone to paedophilia and that sex education in schools is...just a smokescreen for the 'sexualization' of children...[and] that 'LGBT ideology' targets religion and endangers the Polish nation" (Korolczuk 2020).

Against this homophobic backdrop, this chapter explores the sociopolitical and cultural context in view of various strategies of protest and advocacy adopted by queer activists in Poland, highlighting the role of student activism

DOI: 10.4324/9781003565871-9

and the creation of refugee spaces for LGBTQ minorities from across the former communist bloc. Poland's internal perception as a peripheral nation vis-à-vis the West has also played a crucial role in shaping its queer activism landscape. The chapter culminates with an examination of the impact of the 2023 parliamentary election, which marked a significant political shift with the rise of a left-leaning, pro-EU coalition, breaking away from the preceding conservative dominance.

Queerness in Polish Language and Push and Pull Factors of Liberalism and Conservatism

The Polish language, deeply intertwined with national identity and historical narratives, serves as a potent battleground for the politics of queerness. The contestation over linguistic norms reveals the broader ideological struggle between liberal and conservative forces in Poland. Under the Law and Justice Party (PiS) government, from 2015 onwards, this struggle has intensified, reflecting broader global trends of rising populism and conservative backlash against liberal values. To be sure, queerness in the Polish language, or "queering linguistics," involves challenging the traditional, heteronormative structures embedded in the language. This challenge is starkly illustrated by the tensions between international linguistic standards, such as those advocated by the United Nations, and the conservative stances of institutions like the Polish Academy of Sciences. For instance, the resistance to adopting gender-neutral pronouns and inclusive language reflects a broader societal resistance to acknowledging and validating LGBTQ identities.

The concept of queerness disrupts the binary thinking that often characterizes Polish linguistic and cultural norms. Linguistic maps, which visually represent the use and distribution of queer language across different regions and demographics, highlight the uneven acceptance and integration of LGBTQ terms and concepts. These maps reveal a correlation between linguistic inclusivity and areas with stronger liberal influences, often urban centers, compared to more conservative rural areas. The ideological tension between liberalism and conservatism in Poland is deeply rooted in the country's historical and sociopolitical context. The PiS government has leveraged populist rhetoric, heavily infused with religious conservatism, to consolidate power. This approach involves framing liberal values, particularly those related to LGBTQ rights, as threats to national identity and traditional family structures. This framing has polarized the society, creating a push-and-pull dynamic where progressive and conservative forces vie for dominance.

During periods of political transition, such as the anticipated shift with the new Donald Tusk-led government, the struggle between liberalization and conservatism becomes particularly pronounced. These transitions are marked by a questioning of objective truth and the manipulation of norms and concepts as tools in the political game. The stakes in these transitions are high, as they impact not only political power but also the lived experiences and rights of marginalized groups, including LGBTQ individuals. In this context, human rights activists and public health officials have made significant strides in addressing issues such as HIV dissemination and trans healthcare, but their efforts are often overshadowed by political rhetoric. The history of these efforts, and the context in which they operate, must be meticulously mapped out to understand the stakes involved fully. This includes examining the role of minority stress (see, for instance, Meyer 2015), and the impact of social networks and homophily on LGBTQ individuals' experiences (McPherson, Smith-Lovin, and Cook 2001). Moreover, the institutional sexual stigma and its effects on collective action among LGBTQ individuals in Eastern Europe, provide critical insights into the challenges faced by these communities in Poland (Górska, Bilewicz, and Winiewski 2017). Furthermore, the European Union Agency for Fundamental Rights' 2014 survey underscores the pervasive discrimination and violence against LGBTQ people, highlighting the urgent need for inclusive policies and societal change. As Poland navigates the complex interplay between globalism and localism (Kuź 2017), the debates and issues surrounding Europeanization become increasingly pertinent. Next, we delve further into these debates, examining how European integration and the adoption of EU norms intersect with Poland's internal ideological struggles, shaping the future of LGBTQ rights and broader societal norms.

The Impact of Poland's Europeanization Process on National Queerness

The process of Europeanization, particularly in the context of the Eastern enlargement, has generated extensive scholarly debate. Initially dominated by a neo-functionalist perspective (see, for instance, Schimmelfennig and Sedelmeier 2004), the focus has since shifted towards a neo-institutionalist approach, emphasizing the role of actors and discourses in shaping institutions. This shift recognizes Europeanization as more than mere implementation of policies; it includes social learning, norm diffusion, and comprehensive policy transfers. As Maxime Forest articulates, "Europeanization, understood as a set of processes at the level of policy making and institutionalization, along with the practices of advocacy and political or social mobilization, is playing an important role in bringing LGBT issues to light in Central and East European countries" (Forest 2018).

The impact of Europeanization varies significantly across different national contexts. Key factors influencing this impact include institutional arrangements inherited from state socialism, the nature of social actors mobilized around these issues, the level of pressure exerted by European institutions, and the broader policy discussions to which these debates are related, such as anti-discrimination policies, family or welfare policies, and civil code reforms (Forest 2018). Thus, research on Europeanization often emphasizes the vertical interactions between Brussels and the member states, focusing on formal institutional politics between elites at both levels (Ayoub 2013).

The reshaping of "intimate citizenship," as further developed through the EU-funded Quality of Gender+ Equality Initiatives in Europe (QUING), has prominently featured reproductive rights within Central and Eastern Europe (Forest 2018). Since 1990, abortion rights have triggered discourses favoring traditional family values and restricting women's participation in the public sphere. These arguments have been repurposed against LGBT rights, invoking fears over the preservation of traditional marriage and the demographic future of the nation (Forest 2018). While anti-discriminatory policies were mandated as part of EU accession, these policies and the associated LGBT rights debates were highly controversial (Forest 2018). Post-accession periods have seen nationalist backlash, including attempts to ban these policies in national constitutions (see, for instance, Buzogány 2008; Kahlina 2015; Slootmaeckers and Sircar 2014). In Poland, the protection of traditional marriage in the national constitution predates formal EU accession: Article 18 places marriage, defined as a union between a man and woman, under the protection of the state, along with the family and motherhood (Article 18 of the Polish Constitution "Konstytucja Rzeczypospolitej Polskiej" 2019).

Civil society organizations, including LGBT groups, have developed at varying speeds across the region due to differing levels of societal opposition and windows of opportunity. In Poland, the strength of traditional, heteronormative values posed significant challenges for incipient LGBT communities. The Catholic Church, with its strong lobbying and social mobilization capacities, has been a resolute opponent. Consequently, the right to assembly has been repeatedly denied to LGBT-focused civil society organizations, and Poland consistently ranks as one of the most homo-negative countries in the Rainbow Europe Index issued by ILGA-Europe.

The EU accession process, rather than endogenous variables, opened limited opportunities to advance LGBT rights by erasing discriminatory provisions from penal codes and transposing EU anti-discrimination directives into domestic legal orders (Forest 2018). However, these opportunities were highly dependent on the path dependency of individual nations (Forest 2006). Europeanization also involves soft instruments and norm diffusion, transforming patterns of collective action. The introduction of EU policies, funding procedures, and calls for expertise has led feminist and LGBTQI organizations to make substantial changes to their agendas, methods of action, and strategic framings. In Poland, LGBT activists made progress in the years leading up to EU accession through innovative campaigns and the founding of the national LGBT organization, Campaign Against Homophobia (Kampania Przeciw Homofobii, KPH). However, the euphoria associated with EU membership was short-lived as hostile political and social opposition emerged (Ayoub 2013).

Studies on the development of gender equality and anti-discrimination policies at the EU/supranational level found significant variations across different contexts (Forest 2006; Röder 2007). These differences were not only time-dependent, with later accessions involving a greater scope of policies to be implemented, but also strongly connected with domestic factors, such as the role of institutions like the Catholic Church and the political and institutional legacy of the last decades of socialism (Caporaso and Jupille 2019). Here, some emphasize the importance of soft power and norm diffusion in Europeanization, suggesting that for policies to be successfully implemented, they must be viewed as legitimate, correspond with the identity of the member state, and resonate with domestic policy (see, for instance, Schimmelfennig and Sedelmeier 2004).

Although LGBT activists commonly draw from the framework of human rights, finding the resonance needed to meaningfully shift local policy and attitudes is exceptionally challenging for a norm that many societies consider unnatural and associate with disgust (Ayoub 2013; Nussbaum 2010). In Poland, CBOS polls in 2001 showed that the vast majority (88%) considered homosexuality a deviation from the norm, with only 5% considering it normal. Interestingly, 47% of those who viewed it as a deviation also believed it should be tolerated ("Komunikat Z Badań: Preferowane I Realizowane Modele życia Rodzinnego," 2019, 3). By 2005, one year after EU accession, 89% still considered homosexuality a deviation, though 55% now opted for toleration. However, this increase in toleration had strictly defined limits, as 78% of respondents opposed the public display of same-sex relationships ("Stosunek Polaków Do Związek Homoseksualnych" 2019, 5).

Poland's lacking response nationally can be attributed to its emergence from transition with little discourse on LGBT issues prior to the EU accession process, during which the state was subject to new EU standards on LGBT rights (Ayoub 2013). Globalization simultaneously reinforces cultural differences while disseminating images and consumer goods that create the appearance of homogenization (Altman 1999, 576). Similarly, Europeanization has impacted the long-term development of the struggle for LGBT rights in Poland, shaping the ongoing debates and the future of queer activism in an increasingly complex political landscape. However, the influence of the conservative Catholic Church had already left a strong impact on Polish society, which we will turn to next.

Religion in Poland: The Catholic Church and Its Influence

To understand the intricate relationship between religion and Polish society, it is essential to recognize the pivotal role of the Catholic Church. The church's influence can be traced to the foundational unit of society—the family (Garbowski 2020, 69). In the Soviet-dominated Eastern Bloc, particularly during the early 1990s, the breakdown of families was widespread, contributing significantly to the region's demoralization. Under communism, both family and religion were targets of state repression and propaganda, which paradoxically strengthened their interconnection in Poland. Cardinal Stefan Wyszyński, a key spiritual leader from the Stalinist era to the rise of the Solidarity movement (Solidarność), prioritized the reinforcement of the family unit, viewing it as essential to the nation's spiritual and material resilience during the post-communist transition.

The Catholic Church's emphasis on traditional family values continued to shape Polish society long after communism's fall (Osa 1997). The reintegration of religious education in public schools and the promotion of marriage over cohabitation are just a few examples of how the church exerted its influence. Despite the economic hardships of the post-communist "shock therapy," which aimed to transition Poland to a market economy, the church's role in fostering what economist Gary Becker termed "human capital" was notable (Becker 2009, 21–23). While the divorce rate increased post-1989, it remained one of the lowest in Europe, and marriage rates stayed high, with a 2019 CBOS survey indicating that only three percent of couples cohabitated outside marriage. For the first time, this survey also noted that one percent of respondents were in same-sex relationships ("Komunikat Z Badań: Preferowane I Realizowane Modele życia Rodzinnego," 2019, 2).

However, this traditional influence has faced significant shifts in recent years. Younger generations, particularly those in large urban centers, are increasingly distancing themselves from the church (Mirosława Grabowska 2018, 171–88). After Poland's EU accession, the focus shifted from basic material needs to more abstract desires for self-worth and identity. This shift was starkly evident in the 2015 parliamentary elections, where the conservative Law and Justice Party (PiS) secured a significant victory, signaling the start of Poland's complex relationship with the EU. The ensuing conflicts between PiS and the European Commission underscored the tension between Poland's quest for sovereignty and the EU's integrationist policies (Mirosława Grabowska 2018, 171–88).

Mirosława Grabowska characterizes Polish Catholicism as an "endorsed" church, enjoying informal recognition and influence within the state's "civil religion" (Mirosława Grabowska 2018, 171–88) The 1997 constitution, while acknowledging non-religious citizens, clearly roots Polish national identity in Christian heritage: "Poland, beholden to our ancestors for their labors, their struggle for independence achieved at great sacrifice, for our culture rooted in the Christian heritage of the Nation" (Porter-Szucs 2011, 200–1). Despite this, religious orthodoxy is not as deeply ingrained in Polish religiosity as it might appear.

Philip Barker notes that while the intertwining of Christianity and national identity is highly regarded in Poland—far more than in Western Europe—there is a generational divide (see Barker 2008). Older Poles maintain higher levels of religious practice, whereas younger Poles, particularly in urban areas, exhibit a growing aversion to the church. CBOS data reveal that in cities with over half a million residents, more than half of school-aged children opt out of religious classes, a trend mirrored, though less pronounced, in rural areas (Garbowski 2020, 80). This urban-rural divide in religiosity also reflects political leanings. Highly religious southeastern regions, strongholds of the Law and Justice Party, often resist progressive social changes, such as LGBTQ rights (Garbowski 2020, 80). Ordo Iuris, a conservative legal organization, exemplifies the close relationship between the church, the state, and civil society. The group has been instrumental in lobbying against "gender ideologies" and advocating for policies aligned with traditional Catholic values, including efforts to establish "LGBT-Ideology Free Zones" and oppose the Istanbul Convention.[1]

The National Freedom Institute, established in 2019, further exemplifies this synergy by channeling state resources to right-wing NGOs, reinforcing conservative narratives and organizational structures (cited Bill 2022). This approach has mobilized a core base of supporters, ensuring the perpetuation of a conservative social hierarchy aligned with the Law and Justice Party's agenda. Despite these efforts, Polish civil society remains diverse and dynamic. Progressive movements, such as the "black protests" against restrictive abortion laws, demonstrate robust grassroots engagement. Independent organizations, like the Great Orchestra of Christmas Help, continue to thrive despite government opposition, highlighting the complexity and resilience of Polish civil society (Bill 2022). Anti-gender rhetoric, a key element of PiS's critique of neoliberal globalism, has also been adopted by neo-fascist groups, combining traditional gender hierarchies with anti-EU sentiments and Islamophobia (Korolczuk 2020). The 2019 "LGBT Charter" adopted by Warsaw Mayor Rafał Trzaskowski from the Civic Coalition, aimed at supporting LGBTQ individuals and combating discrimination, triggered a significant backlash, further illustrating the deep-seated cultural and political divides in Poland (Ciobanu 2020).

In summary, the Catholic Church's historical and ongoing influence in Poland shapes the nation's cultural and political landscape. While traditional values remain strong, particularly in rural areas, urban centers and younger generations are increasingly challenging the church's dominance, leading to a complex and evolving dynamic between religion, politics, and society. Rooted deeply in Polish identity, the Church has been a significant force in politics, particularly in promoting conservative values. The Church's opposition to LGBTQ rights, framed as a defense of traditional family structures and moral values, has been a cornerstone of its influence, reinforcing the cultural conservatism prevalent in Polish society.

In this context, the rise of new conservatism post-2015 has further entrenched these values. PiS has capitalized on this cultural backdrop, amplifying anti-LGBTQ rhetoric and policies to galvanize its voter base. This strategy has been starkly visible in PiS's legislative and media campaigns, such as the controversial documentary "Invasion," which portrayed LGBTQ rights as a foreign threat to Polish values and children, equating it to historical invasions and communism (Cienski 2019; Magdalena Grabowska and Rawłuszko 2021). This environment has paved the way for far-right entities like the Konfederacja Party, which emerged in 2019 with an agenda explicitly targeting LGBTQ communities. Konfederacja's rhetoric, including proposals for anti-LGBTQ laws and inflammatory statements by its leaders, underscores a shift towards more extreme conservative ideologies. Their platform, encapsulated in the "Konfederacja Five," reflects a broader societal resistance to progressive values, driven by fears of sociocultural change and the loss of traditional power structures (Cienski 2019; Magdalena Grabowska and Rawłuszko 2021). The convergence of the Church's influence and the rise of new conservatism illustrates a political landscape where LGBTQ rights are not merely a cultural issue but a pivotal battleground for Poland's identity and values. This interplay has solidified a conservative bloc that leverages fear and traditionalism to maintain its grip on power, often at the expense of minority rights and progressive reforms. We look at the development of this conservative trend in recent years.

The New Conservatism: From PiS to the Far Right Post-2015

During a September 2019 press conference in Lublin, Witold Tumanowicz, a candidate for the newly formed Konfederacja Party, articulated the party's stance on LGBT issues, stating their intention "to fight for the separation of LGBT and the state. We are going to pass an anti-LGBT law … to make sure that public spaces are free from provocative symbols and behaviors" (Aleksowska 2019). Though Tumanowicz was not elected, Konfederacja secured nearly seven percent of the vote in the 2019 parliamentary elections, a significant achievement for a party formally registered just two months prior in July 2019.

In a May 2019 lecture, Sławomir Mentzen, then-head of Konfederacja in Pomerania, outlined the party's five core postulates, known as the "Konfederacja Five": "We don't want Jews, homosexuals, abortion, taxes, and the European Union" (Sitnicka 2019). This explicit articulation of far-right sentiment highlighted the party's broad agenda against various minority groups and progressive policies. Grzegorz Braun, leader of the Korona Party, an affiliate of Konfederacja, was noted for inflammatory remarks such as advocating for the whipping of homosexuals, which, according to Tumanowicz, increased the party's support.

Konfederacja representatives criticized the PiS party for not taking stronger action against what they termed leftist "gender" and "LGBT" ideology. Tumanowicz highlighted the dismissal of a county school superintendent who had made homophobic remarks on national television, calling it an example of PiS's "hypocrisy towards the Left and LGBT ideology." Marek Szewczyk, another Konfederacja candidate, warned that without parental opposition, "we would have a rainbow propaganda festival in primary school" (PAP 2020).

A notable example of PiS's anti-LGBT campaign leading up to the 2019 parliamentary election was the airing of the documentary film "Invasion"

(Inwazja) on public television channel TVP. The film, aired on the eve of the elections, claimed to expose the "background, aims, method and money of the LGBT 'invasion' in Poland" through undercover reporting at pride marches. LGBT rights activists were depicted as a "foreign-backed threat to Polish children, religion, values, and the very biological continuation of the nation" (Ambroziak 2019). This narrative aligns with what scholars like Grzebalska and Pető have termed the "securitization" of NGOs, where certain topics and organizations are framed as existential threats, moving them outside the realm of regular politics. The documentary drew historical parallels between LGBT activism and invasions like the Swedish Deluge of the 17th century and more recent German and Russian occupations, suggesting that the acceptance of LGBT ideology would lead to greater societal degradation than the worst excesses of communism. It claimed that if the "rainbow revolution" continued unchecked, it would eventually normalize pedophilia (Ambroziak 2019).

This anti-LGBT rhetoric appeared to resonate with certain demographics. A September 2019 survey by *Gazeta Wyborcza* found that while most women under 40 viewed the "climate crisis" as the greatest threat, the majority of men in the same age group saw "gender ideology and the LGBT movement" as the primary concern (Wantuch 2019). This trend mirrors the rise of conservative ideologies among young men, contrasted with the leftward shift among young women, exemplified by the mass mobilization against the proposed blanket ban on abortion in 2016 (Walker 2019).

As Elżbieta Korolczuk notes, "anti-gender campaigns" in Poland have effectively facilitated the electoral victory of right-wing parties and continuously mobilized specific groups, particularly young men and older, deeply religious voters (Korolczuk 2020, 167). These groups form the base of far-right, neo-fascist, and populist parties like PiS and Konfederacja and are the most susceptible to anti-gender ideology discourse. Data indicate that right-wing populist and far-right parties strategically and opportunistically adopt anti-gender rhetoric to exploit the anxieties and hopes of groups experiencing relative deprivation and precarity, as well as those fearing sociocultural change and the loss of power and status (Korolczuk 2020). The ongoing success of parties like PiS and *Konfederacja* suggests a strategic use of anti-LGBT and anti-gender rhetoric to solidify their support base and influence public discourse, reflecting broader trends in European far-right movements. This has also led to a broader neocolonial perception of Brussels influence on Polish society and culture, redefining the notion of Europeanization.

Europeanization Reframed: "Neo-colonialism" from Brussels

When viewed through the lens of domestic impact, Europeanization can be interpreted in various ways by national and subnational actors. Woll and Jacquot (2010), for instance, investigated how EU accession has influenced policy-building and the diverse uses of the concept of "Europe" among these actors.

These interpretations range from seeing Europe as a historical actor disconnected from EU institutions, to viewing the EU as a legitimizer and a political and social trendsetter, and even as a threat to national values and interests (Rozenberg 2007). In fact, the perception of the EU as a "threat to national values and interests" has gained significant traction, particularly within right-wing political organizations. Grzegorz Braun, leader of *Korona* mentioned above, articulated this view by stating that *Konfederacja* "stands for the security of the state and of human life in the Polish state, for the security of faith, a normal family...Christian tradition and civilization must be defended against the rainbow revolution, against the influence of foreign empires, foreign embassies" (Aleksowska 2019). This perspective goes beyond the faith-family nation triad often espoused by ultraconservatives worldwide, framing the EU's influence as a form of neo-colonialism (Aleksowska 2019).

In Poland, two competing discourses have emerged regarding the viability of same-sex partnerships. One discourse, rooted in the values of equality, non-discrimination, respect for human rights, and the protection of minorities, aligns with the principles of the EU Charter. The other discourse, however, frames EU influence as a form of cultural imposition that threatens traditional Polish values. Historically, the EU's impact on Poland has been perceived primarily in terms of economic benefits rather than social policy or human rights (Szczerbiak 2007). This perception has been exploited by Eurosceptic conservative parties like Law and Justice (PiS), which have framed the debate as an issue of EU (German/Brussels) "colonization" (Petras 2016).

The longstanding conservatism of Polish society further complicates the reception of EU influence. This conservatism provides fertile ground for the rhetoric of right-wing parties, which portray Europeanization as a threat to Poland's cultural and national identity. By positioning themselves as defenders of traditional values against the supposed encroachments of a foreign, liberal agenda, these parties gain support from segments of the population wary of rapid sociocultural changes. The discourse around Europeanization in Poland, therefore, is not just about policy alignment with the EU but also about the broader cultural and ideological implications. It reflects a struggle over national identity, sovereignty, and the extent to which Poland should integrate with broader European norms and values. This ongoing debate highlights the complexities of Europeanization in a country where historical, cultural, and political factors intersect in multifaceted ways.

Resilient Activism in Poland: Within and Beyond National Boundaries

The spread of LGBT acceptance across European societies is critically influenced by transnational activism. Domestic actors embedded in transnational networks play an essential role in advancing acceptance in their home countries. In fact, these transnational actors mediate between international and domestic norms, framing messages to fit local contexts and addressing perceptions of threats associated with LGBT norms (Ayoub 2013). This "local framing" is tied to the concept of "norm visibility," which is the relative ability of public and governments to see and interact with ideas and images that define standards of appropriate behavior (Ayoub 2013). Building on Altman's thesis about globalization's impact on sexuality (Altman 1999, 559–84), the Polish case thus also succumbs to the issue that globalization creates a set of new standards of acceptability, which often conflict with traditional mores (Ayoub 2013).

Suffice it to say that, however, that Europeanization significantly impacted LGBT activism by facilitating the development of transnational networks between member states, exemplified by the relationship between Germany and Poland (Ayoub 2013). This dynamic is particularly evident in the case of the illegal 2005 Equality March (Parada Równości) in Warsaw. The "abundance of social spaces" and "organization resources" in neighboring Germany were critical variables in bringing together key actors, defining their common identity, and empowering them with necessary resources (Princen and Kerremans 2008, 1131–2). Berlin, with its large Polish expat community, geographic proximity, history as a "gay capital," and the impact of Europeanization, played an essential role in fostering activism in Poland. This transnational cooperation was vital given the comparative lack of social and organizational capital in post-communist Poland. Around the time of the 2005 Equality March, there were significantly more LGBT organizations active in Berlin than in Warsaw, underscoring the disparity in organizational infrastructure.

Domestic organizations in Poland, while bolstered by increased mobility and external social capital due to Europeanization, continue to play a crucial role in activism. Supranational umbrella organizations like ILGA-Europe are well-equipped for formal lobbying, but domestic organizations engage more broadly in the public sphere, providing "mobilizing structures" such as family units, friendship networks, voluntary associations, and even elements of the state structure that promote activism (Lang 2009). Public mobilization alongside formal advocacy work is equally important, as LGBT activism is geared towards both society and the state (Ayoub 2013). Hence, domestic Polish organizations maintain strong connections in Europe, both horizontally and vertically. For instance, a significant portion of the funding for KPH (the largest Polish LGBT organization) comes from international sources, and foreign embassies in Poland fund many local LGBT campaigns. However, transnational activists face challenges related to the strong presence of the Catholic Church and fears of tapping into the deep-seated mythology of national martyrdom, which is strengthened by historical memories of World War II.

Transnational Linkages and Polish Grassroots

Transnational activists in Poland had to navigate the dual challenge of addressing both sexual deviance and German influence, as Polish nationalism is largely grounded in Catholic values and anti-German sentiment (Ayoub 2013). This fear was evident during the 2005 Equality March, where activists were concerned that too many Germans attending would feed into the propaganda that Germans aimed to destroy Polish values. To be sure, Poland has seen a diverse array of responses to rising anti-LGBT rhetoric and attempted legislation, ranging from legislative efforts to grassroots initiatives. These efforts include art installations and exhibitions, such as the "Queer Archives Institute," founded by artist Karol Radziszewski in 2015, which focuses on queer art endeavors in Central and Eastern Europe.[2] Dialogues between queer curators and artists, like the 2018 event "Identity, Erotica, and Politics: LGBTQ Art Now!" hosted in Poznań, have also contributed to the movement ("Tożsamość, erotyka i polityka – sztuka LGBTQ teraz! - Galeria Miejska Arsenał w Poznaniu" 2017). In this context, popular culture has played a role as well, with films like the 2021 "Operation Hyacinth" (Hiacynt) receiving critical acclaim and awards (Ciaston 2021). Video campaigns, such as a queer Polish couple's YouTube channel lip-synching popular songs, including Taylor Swift's "You Need to Calm Down," have brought visibility to the cause. This video featured notable queer Polish political figures and highlighted the issue of "LGBT-free zones."[3]

The online map service "Atlas nienawiści" (Atlas of Hate) tracks locations of "LGBT-free zones" across Poland, demonstrating the extent of discriminatory policies.[4] National and local LGBT-equality organizations, such as *Love Does Not Exclude* (Miłość nie Wyklucza), founded in 2009, and student organizations like "Queer UW" at the University of Warsaw, have been instrumental in promoting equality. These organizations have inspired similar groups to form across Poland, including in Poznań, Opole, Wrocław, and Łódź. International initiatives, like *Queering the Map* (further in our next chapter), a web-based atlas allowing users to geotag locations with personalized messages, show a broader range of activity than conventional urban-based activism might reveal. These initiatives occupy the "in-between" spaces discussed in earlier chapters, bridging local and transnational efforts to advance LGBT rights and acceptance in Poland.

The Rise of Queer Student Activism and its Role in Conservative-Leaning Poland

Queer activism in Poland has emerged as a potent force challenging the country's repressive and conservative state politics. The rise of organizations like *TęczUJ*, the first LGBTQ student association at Jagiellonian University, exemplifies this grassroots resistance. These groups advocate for LGBTQ rights in an environment where the ruling Law and Justice Party (PiS) and the Catholic Church wield significant influence, often promoting anti-LGBTQ rhetoric and policies. This hostile climate includes "LGBT-free zones" and aggressive political campaigns portraying LGBTQ rights as threats to national identity (Bogatyrev and Bogusz 2024; Wanat 2020).

Despite these challenges, queer activism has not only persisted but also grown more visible and resilient. The violent attacks on pride marches in 2019 led to a robust online campaign, #jestemLGBT, which increased the visibility of LGBTQ individuals and highlighted the community's resilience (Bogatyrev and Bogusz 2024). Additionally, the number of pride events has steadily increased, with 37 independent marches taking place in 2023, reflecting a shift in public attitudes towards greater acceptance and support for LGBTQ rights (Bogatyrev and Bogusz 2024). Activists have strategically built alliances with other social movements, emphasizing intersectionality and solidarity. For instance, LGBTQ groups have joined forces with feminist and pro-refugee activists, demonstrating a unified front against broader social injustices (Magdalena Grabowska and Rawłuszko 2021). This collaborative approach not only strengthens the LGBTQ movement but also amplifies its impact by integrating it into a wider struggle for human rights and democracy. However, the path remains fraught with challenges. Political figures often exploit LGBTQ issues for electoral gain, using divisive tactics to rally conservative bases while sidelining LGBTQ rights in broader political discourse (Cienski 2019; Wanat 2020). Despite some progress in public opinion and increased visibility, structural barriers and political hostility continue to impede full equality.

As queer student activism in Poland rises against the tide of conservative politics, creating visible and resilient movements, the landscape of LGBTQ rights in other parts of Europe tells a different story. While Poland navigates its own challenges with shifting political dynamics, Russia faces even more severe repression. The autocratic regime in Russia, amidst its ongoing war in Ukraine, has intensified its scapegoating of LGBTQ communities, framing them as politically subversive and pro-Western. This has led to heightened persecution and state-condoned violence, pushing queer activism into an underground mode of survival. The next chapter delves into these harsh realities, exploring the strategies and resilience of Russian LGBTQ advocacy in the face of systemic oppression and political violence.

Notes

1 (For an overview of the 2019 Sejm and Senate results in Poland "Wybory do Sejmu i Senatu Rzeczypospolitej Polskiej 2019 r," n.d., For a map of the communities that featured "LGBT-Ideology Free Zones" as of July 2020, see "Gminy Wolne Od LGBT". Zobacz, Gdzie Są W Polsce [MAPY]" 2020).
2 Queer Archives Institute, accessed from: http://queerarchivesinstitute.org.
3 Accessed from: https://youtu.be/5QmecWS8OFM.
4 See website at https://atlasnienawisci.pl/, accessed 13 July 2024.

References

Aleksowska, Blanka. 2019. "Konfederacja: Rozdzielimy LGBT od państwa. Wprowadzimy ustawę anty-LGBT." DoRzeczy.pl. September 29, 2019. https://dorzeczy.pl/kraj/115550/konfederacja-wprowadzimy-ustawe-anty-lgbt.html

Altman, D. 1999. "Globalization, Political Economy, and HIV/AIDS." *Theory and Society* 28 (4): 559–84.

Ambroziak, Anton. 2019. "TVP o Inwazji LGBT: „Potop", "gorsza niż najbardziej zagorzali komuniści", "czeka nas legalizacja pedofilii"." OKO.press. October 11, 2019. https://oko.press/tvp-o-inwazji-lgbt-potop-gorsza-niz-najbardziej-zagorzali-komunisci-czeka-nas-legalizacja-pedofilii

Ayoub, Phillip M. 2013. "Cooperative Transnationalism in Contemporary Europe: Europeanization and Political Opportunities for LGBT Mobilization in the European Union." *European Political Science Review* 5 (2): 279–310.

Barker, P. 2008. "Religious Nationalism in Modern Europe: If God Be for Us," August. https://doi.org/10.4324/9780203892848

Becker, Gary S. 2009. *Human Capital: A Theoretical and Empirical Analysis, with Special Reference to Education.* Chicago, IL: University of Chicago Press.

Bill, Stanley. 2022. "Counter-Elite Populism and Civil Society in Poland: PiS's Strategies of Elite Replacement." *Eastern European Politics and Societies: EEPS* 36 (1): 118–40.

Bogatyrev, Konstantin, and Honorata Bogusz. 2024. "On the Verge of Progress? LGBTQ+ Politics in Poland after the 2023 Elections." *European Journal of Politics and Gender* 1 (aop): 1–7.

Buzogány, Aron. 2008. "Joining Europe, Not Sodom: LGBT Rights and the Limits of Europeanization in Hungary and Romania." In *National Convention of the American Association for the Advancement of Slavic Studies (AAASS)*, 20–23.

Caporaso, James, and Joseph Jupille. 2019. "2. The Europeanization of Gender Equality Policy and Domestic Structural Change." In *Transforming Europe*, edited by Maria Green Cowles, James Caporaso, and Thomas Risse, 21–43. Ithaca, NY: Cornell University Press.

Ciaston, Marcin. 2021. *Operation Hyacinth (2021)* ★ *6.8 | Crime, Drama.* https://www.imdb.com/title/tt14315584/

Cienski, Jan. 2019. "Gay Pride Gets Political in Poland." POLITICO. August 10, 2019. https://www.politico.eu/article/gay-pride-and-polish-politics/

Ciobanu, Claudia. 2020. "A Third of Poland Declared 'LGBT-Free Zone.'" Balkan Insight. BIRN. February 25, 2020. https://balkaninsight.com/2020/02/25/a-third-of-poland-declared-lgbt-free-zone/

Forest, Maxime. 2006. "Emerging Gender Interest Groups in the New Member States: The Case of the Czech Republic." *Perspectives on European Politics and Society* 7 (2): 170–84.

Forest, Maxime. 2018. "Europeanizing vs. Nationalizing the Issue of Same-Sex Marriage in Central Europe: A Comparative Analysis of Framing Processes in Croatia, Hungary, Slovakia, and Slovenia." In *Global Perspectives on Same-Sex Marriage*, 127–48. Cham: Springer International Publishing.

Garbowski, Christopher. 2020. "Catholicism in the New Poland: A Religion and Society in Transition." *Occasional Papers on Religion in Eastern Europe* 40 (5): 6.

"Gminy Wolne Od LGBT". Zobacz, Gdzie Są W Polsce [MAPY]." 2020. Uhlig, Dominik; Bartosz Chyż. July 15, 2020. https://biqdata.wyborcza.pl/biqdata/7,159116,26130986,gminy-wolne-od-lgbt-zobacz-gdzie-sa-w-polsce-mapy.html

Górska, Paulina, Michał Bilewicz, and Mikołaj Winiewski. 2017. "Invisible to the State. Institutional Sexual Stigma and Collective Action of LGB Individuals in Five East European Countries." *Group Processes & Intergroup Relations* 20 (3): 367–81.

Grabowska, Magdalena, and Marta Rawłuszko. 2021. "Everyday Feminism and the Authoritarian Right in Poland." Heinrich Böll Stiftung. December 1, 2021. https://www.boell.de/en/2021/12/01/everyday-feminism-and-authoritarian-right-poland

Grabowska, Mirosława. 2018. "Bóg a sprawa polska. Poza granicami teorii sekularyzacji." https://www.ceeol.com/search/book-detail?id=845447

Kahlina, Katja. 2015. "Local Histories, European LGBT Designs: Sexual Citizenship, Nationalism, and 'Europeanisation' in Post-Yugoslav Croatia and Serbia." *Women's Studies International Forum* 49 (March):73–83.

"Komunikat Z Badań: Preferowane I Realizowane Modele życia Rodzinnego." 2019. Centrum Badania Opinii Społecznej. https://www.cbos.pl/SPISKOM.POL/2019/K_046_19.PDF

"Konstytucja Rzeczypospolitej Polskiej." 2019. https://www.sejm.gov.pl/prawo/konst/polski/1.htm

Korolczuk, E. 2020. "The Fight against 'gender'and 'LGBT Ideology': New Developments in Poland." *European Journal of Politics and Gender* 3 (1): 165–67.

Kuź, Michał. 2017. "Globalism and Localism in the Perspective of Polish Politics." *The Warsaw Institute Review*.

Lang, S. 2009. "Assessing Advocacy: European Transnational Women's Networks and Gender Mainstreaming." *Social Politics* 16 (3): 327–57.

McPherson, Miller, Lynn Smith-Lovin, and James M. Cook. 2001. "Birds of a Feather: Homophily in Social Networks." *Annual Review of Sociology* 27 (1): 415–44.

Meyer, I. 2015. "Resilience in the Study of Minority Stress and Health of Sexual and Gender Minorities." *Psychology of Sexual Orientation and Gender Diversity* 2 (3): 209–13.

Nussbaum, Martha C. 2010. *From Disgust to Humanity: Sexual Orientation and Constitutional Law*. London: Oxford University Press.

Osa, Maryjane. 1997. "Creating Solidarity: The Religious Foundations of the Polish Social Movement." *Eastern European Politics and Societies: EEPS* 11 (2): 339–65.

PAP. 2020. "Konfederacja zarzuca PiS hipokryzję w sprawie LGBT." PTWP-ONLINE Sp. z o.o. August 24, 2020. https://www.wnp.pl/parlamentarny/spoleczenstwo/konfederacja-zarzuca-pis-hipokryzje-w-sprawie-lgbt,92748.html.

Petras, James. 2016. *The End of the Republic and the Delusion of Empire*. Atlanta: Clarity Press. https://books.google.com/books?hl=en&lr=&id=t4pXDwAAQBAJ&oi=fnd&pg=PT7&dq=++Petras+2015+colonial+poland&ots=AYqICKbfOa&sig=zPlL9efOoDr0wjz0wZK_IlYv-0c

Porter-Szucs, B. 2011. *Faith and Fatherland: Catholicism, Modernity, and Poland*. Oxford: Oxford University Press.

Princen, Sebastiaan, and Bart Kerremans. 2008. "Opportunity Structures in the EU Multi-Level System." *West European Politics* 31 (6): 1129–46.

Röder, I. 2007. "Gender Equality, Pre-Accession Assistance and Europeanisation: Two Post-Socialist Countries on Their Way to the European Union."

Rozenberg, Olivier. 2007. "L'enjeu Européen Dans Les Transformations Postcommunistes: Hongrie, Pologne, République Tchèque, 1989-2004," 183–87.

Schimmelfennig, Frank, and Ulrich Sedelmeier. 2004. "Governance by Conditionality: EU Rule Transfer to the Candidate Countries of Central and Eastern Europe." *Journal of European Public Policy* 11 (4): 661–79.

Sitnicka, Dominika. 2019. "'Nie chcemy Żydów, gejów, aborcji, podatków i UE. To trafia do wyborców' [PIĄTKA KONFEDERACJI]." OKO.press. May 1, 2019. https://oko.press/program-konfederacji-zydzi-geje-aborcja.

Slootmaeckers, Koen, and I. Sircar. 2014. "Croatia, the EU, and the Marriage Referendum: The Symbolic Case of LGBT Rights," September. https://scholar.google.com/citations?user=L22QuEwAAAAJ&hl=en&oi=sra

"Stosunek Polaków Do Związek Homoseksualnych." 2019. Centrum Badania Opinii Społecznej. https://www.cbos.pl/SPISKOM.POL/2019/K_090_19.PDF

Szczerbiak, Aleks. 2007. "'Social Poland' Defeats 'Liberal Poland'? The September–October 2005 Polish Parliamentary and Presidential Elections." *Journal of Communist Studies and Transition Politics* 23 (2): 203–32.

"Tożsamość, erotyka i polityka – sztuka LGBTQ teraz! - Galeria Miejska Arsenał w Poznaniu." 2017. Galeria Miejska Arsenał w Poznaniu - Galeria Sztuki Współczesnej/ Gallery of Contemporary Art. Galeria Miejska Arsenał w Poznaniu. December 28, 2017. https://arsenal.art.pl/event/tozsamosc-erotyka-i-polityka-sztuka-lgbtq-teraz/

Walker, Shaun. 2019. "Poland's Drift to Right Divides Young Male and Female Voters." *The Guardian*, October 8, 2019. https://www.theguardian.com/world/2019/oct/08/poland-election-drift-to-right-divides-young-male-and-female-voters

Wanat, Zosia. 2020. "Poland's LGBTQ Community in the Political Crosshairs." POLITICO. June 19, 2020. https://www.politico.eu/article/poland-lgbtq-community-in-the-political-crosshairs-elections-duda/

Wantuch, Dominika. 2019. "Ideologia gender jest szkodliwa." wyborcza.pl. September 14, 2019. https://classic.wyborcza.pl/archiwumGW/9168595/Ideologia-gender-jest-szkodliwa

Woll, Cornelia, and Sophie Jacquot. 2010. "Using Europe: Strategic Action in Multi-Level Politics." *Comparative European Politics* 8 (1): 110–26.

"Wybory do Sejmu i Senatu Rzeczypospolitej Polskiej 2019 r." n.d. Accessed July 29, 2024. https://sejmsenat2019.pkw.gov.pl/sejmsenat2019/

7 Queer Scapegoating in Russia

In our previous chapter, we concluded with some reflections on the impact of the changing political landscape on queer rights following the 2023 parliamentary election in Poland. We notably underscored how a left-leaning, pro-EU coalition broke with the overarching conservatism of the previous government. This chapter takes the opposite approach, focusing on the effects of repressive politics in the context of autocratic regimes fueling political violence to distract from existential regime threats. While examples are abundant, including Africa and Asia, we chose the case of Russia to create a selection of empirical studies that provide a narrative flow between the samples. To be sure, the current war in Ukraine has heightened the challenges the Russian government faces to maintain its domestic social order. One of the discursive and political practices by the regime is a scapegoating campaign against LGBTQ communities, viewed by the authorities as engaging in politically subversive, pro-Western behaviors. Increased persecution and state-condoned violence have rendered the situation for queer activism and causes challenging, pushing it into a resilience-driven underground mode of operation to survive. The authors map current conditions and responses by advocacy groups and stakeholders in these difficult and uncertain times.

The Slippery Slope from Illiberal Democracies to Autocratic Regimes

Before delving into the intricacies of the Russian case, it is helpful to compare some of our previous Polish experiences against the backdrop of queerness in the Soviet and post-Soviet context, as it provides us with a more nuanced understanding of how illiberal democracies and repressive regimes shape the experiences and struggles of LGBTQ communities. Both regions have witnessed significant repression, yet their histories and socio-political dynamics offer distinct contexts for these challenges.

DOI: 10.4324/9781003565871-10

Ideological Foundations

The Soviet Union's ideological framework, particularly under Stalin, was grounded in Socialist Realism, which aimed to construct the ideal "New Soviet Man" and excluded non-heteronormative identities. Homosexuality was criminalized, viewed as a disease, and subjected to severe repression and invisibility (Essig 1999; Mitchell 2016). This ideological stance persisted into post-Soviet Russia, where Vladimir Putin's regime has reinforced heteropatriarchal nationalism, idealizing white ethnic Russian heteronormativity and aligning national identity with traditional values (Davydova 2019).

In Poland, the ideological opposition to LGBTQ rights is deeply intertwined with religious conservatism, particularly the influence of the Catholic Church. The notion of "gender ideology" has been weaponized by right-wing factions to oppose various gender and sexual equality initiatives, portraying LGBTQ rights as a threat to the traditional family, the nation, and Christian civilization. This rhetoric mirrors American anti-gay rights campaigns of the 1970s, spreading misinformation about LGBTQ individuals (Afshar 2006). While we expand on the historical context of queerness in Russia in our next section, it is essential to briefly touch on some of the legal and social repression in both the Soviet/Russian and Polish contexts.

Legal and Social Repression and the Role of Activism

In Soviet Russia, legal measures criminalized homosexuality, and cultural censorship further suppressed LGBTQ visibility. Post-Soviet Russia saw the implementation of repressive laws, such as the "gay propaganda" law of 2013, which increased legal and social discrimination against LGBTQ individuals. These laws have forced LGBTQ people to adopt survival strategies, such as selective coming out and emigration preparation (Zhabenko 2019). Poland's legal framework also institutionalizes discrimination against LGBTQ individuals. The national constitution enshrines traditional marriage, and right-wing factions have successfully mobilized to resist progressive reforms. Despite EU-driven anti-discrimination policies, implementation has been uneven, and the Catholic Church's lobbying power remains a formidable obstacle (Siegel 2020).

Despite significant repression, LGBTQ activism in Russia has persisted through alternative methods. Activists often use social media, petitions, and educational initiatives to advocate for their rights, minimizing direct confrontation with authorities. This form of invisible activism is seen as more sustainable and safer in the face of state repression (Levitanus and Kislitsyna 2024). In Poland, LGBTQ activism has also shown resilience, leveraging European norms and funding to advance their cause. Organizations like the Campaign Against Homophobia (KPH) have implemented innovative campaigns, but progress is met with significant resistance from conservative forces. The influence of the EU has been crucial in opening some opportunities for LGBTQ advocacy. Yet deeply ingrained cultural opposition persists as the struggle for an EU identity is intertwined with a larger queer logic across the EU space (Eigenmann 2022).

European Influence and Contemporary Issues

Russia's antagonistic stance toward Western values and norms has further entrenched its repressive policies. Western perceptions have historically constructed Russia as the sexual "other," influencing both internal and external narratives about LGBTQ rights. This dynamic complicates the discourse around LGBTQ issues in Russia, as political homophobia is not merely an opposition to Western values but is entangled in broader nationalist projects (Baer 2016; Suchland 2018). The European Union plays a pivotal role in shaping LGBTQ rights in Poland, offering both opportunities and constraints. Europeanization has facilitated some progress by mandating anti-discrimination policies, but these policies are controversial and often face nationalist backlash. The process of Europeanization involves not just policy directives but also norm diffusion and social learning, which interact with domestic factors such as the influence of the Catholic Church and the legacy of socialism (Ramet 2019).

As the empirical discussion drawing on specific Russian cases and social media analysis later in this chapter demonstrates, the future of LGBTQ rights in Russia is uncertain and heavily dependent on broader political and social developments. Ongoing repression under Putin's regime poses significant challenges to LGBTQ activism. The resilience and adaptability of activists will be crucial in shaping the future of queer rights in the region. As mentioned in our previous chapter, Poland's recent political shift toward a pro-EU coalition offers a potential turning point for LGBTQ rights. However, deeply ingrained cultural and religious opposition remains a significant barrier. The evolving political landscape and the influence of European norms will play a critical role in determining the future of queer rights in Poland. Before turning our attention to specific case illustrations, we provide readers with an overview of the historical and primarily chronological account of queerness and their rights within tsarist Russia, the Soviet Union and contemporary Russian society.

A Brief Chronology of Queerness in Russia

A chronology of queerness and LGBT rights in Russia is best examined by a brief overview of the distinct political structures that defined Russian history. These periods range from the Tsarist Russian Empire, and the Communist-ruled Soviet Union, to the current post-USSR authoritarian era. This broad demarcation showcases how queer rights are intertwined with the prevailing political goals of each structure, where top-down initiatives often portray homosexuality as a subversive element threatening the survival of Russian society.

In the Russian Empire, attitudes toward homosexuality were often contradictory and inconsistently expressed. Tsar Nicholas I had passed Article 995 in 1832, making sodomy a criminal act punishable by exile to Siberia for five years. The law did not cover female homosexuality, or other sexual acts beyond sodomy between men. Thus, anti-homosexual attitudes were inconsistently expressed with enforcement dependent on factors such as one's standing with the Imperial family and social status.

Following the Russian Revolution and the transition to the Bolshevik government, the 1832 tsarist law on homosexuality was repealed, and no equivalent articles were introduced in the first Soviet Russian Criminal Code of 1922 (Mole 2020, 1). However, this does not paint a complete picture of how non-heteronormative behavior was perceived in Communist Russia. Amidst a period of great upheaval, citizens were expected to prioritize collective interest over individual desire, and "homosexuality was soon reconceived as abnormal ... and contrary to the public good" (Mole 2020, 2). This strengthened the association of homosexuality with "decadent bourgeois morality" intertwining sexuality with class issues (Mole 2020, 2). Soviet Commissar for Justice, Nikolai Krylenko, proclaimed in the early 1930s that" there was no reason for anyone to be homosexual," viewing it as a leftover of the exploiting class (cited in Mole 2020, 2).

This initial post-revolution progress for queer rights was quickly overturned as Stalin consolidated his power. Homosexual behavior was criminalized in 1933 and punishable for up to five years in prison under Article 121.1 of the Soviet criminal law, including voluntary sodomy. Lesbian relations were not officially criminalized, resulting instead in incarceration in psychiatric institutions (Rivkin-Fish and Hartblay 2014, 99). As Justine Kerf notes, "gay men were sent to the gulag along with political dissidents, strengthening the criminal connotation" (Kerf 2017, 137). Queer visibility as an implication that the socialist revolution had failed "to eradicate the lingering influence of the bourgeoisie," making it imperative to render homosexuals invisible (Mole 2020, 2).

The fall of the Soviet Union in the 1990s brought new dilemmas. As repression gave way to a sudden democratic opening, society reconsidered how previously invisible queer communities would fit into the post-Soviet Russian state. Initial attempts to signal a more tolerant Russia still failed to rectify societal prejudices consolidated under Stalin. In 1993, "consenting sexual acts between adult men were decriminalized in a bid to facilitate Russia's membership of the Council of Europe - but it was on the understanding that gays and lesbians would remain out of sight" (Mole 2020, 3). In what Richard C. M. Mole calls the "sexual contract", LGBT Russians were still "expected to remain invisible" in a state where public spaces were implicitly reserved for heterosexual citizens

(Mole 2020, 3). This occurred as freedom of speech and censorship laws were being overhauled, creating intense existential pressures across society (Rivkin-Fish and Hartblay 2014, 101). The democratization effort included the rise of an influential oligarch class via industrial privatization and complications from the Chechen War. Democracy became associated with "instability, corruption, and fraud," setting the stage for a political strongman (Kerf 2017, 37).

Vladimir Putin fulfilled this role, initially guiding the state to economic growth. However, growing authoritarianism, oligarchism, and re-centralization of power under Putin led to public discontent, evident in the mass protests following the 2011 elections. The LGBTQ community became a scapegoat with Putin opposing Western values and portraying gays and lesbians as representatives of Western influence (Kerf 2017, 38). State-sponsored homophobia linked queer Russians to foreign perversion, reinforcing Putin's anti-West credentials. This aimed to consolidate heteronormative standards and "remasculinize Russia" (Mole 2020, 4), framing queer individuals as state enemies (Rivkin-Fish and Hartblay 2014, 102).

meant that popular discontent would manifest once again. This was evident in the mass protests following the 2011 elections, where public opposition to Putin was clear. Under these conditions, it becomes clear why the LGBT community has been heavily targeted in post-Soviet Russia. De Kerf notes that "the Kremlin needed a clear-cut enemy against whom Putin could vigorously protect Russia and its values... Putin wanted to oppose Western values. In Russia, 'no one represents Western influence and otherness better than gays and lesbians'" (Kerf 2017, 38). Repression of queer Russians therefore becomes a politically expedient strategy to both minimize internal opposition, as well as pander to Putin's supporters by buttressing his anti-West credentials. In creating a direct link between Western perversion and queer Russians, state-sponsored homophobia regurgitated the familiar rhetoric of otherness and foreign importation. Given Putin's recurring obsession with restoring Russian national pride, Richard Mole highlights the interplay between political goals and sexual rights, where the consolidation of heteronormative standards is intended to reflect the "remasculinization of Russia" (Mole 2020, 4). Queer individuals, groups, and organizations are therefore easily reframed as enemies of the state, threatening its very existence through the disruption of the societal ideals for masculine and feminine roles, the uprooting of religious beliefs, and sparking fears of reproductive rates declining (Rivkin-Fish and Hartblay 2014, 102).

The 2013 "gay propaganda law" allows fines "for disseminating information about 'non-traditional sexual orientations' among minors, promoting 'the social equivalence of traditional and non-traditional relationships,'" or depicting homosexuals as role models (Mole 2020, 5). This law stifles opposition, in incentivizing non-heteronormative citizens to remain invisible. Efforts by external advocacy groups must incorporate Russian LGBTQ voices to address injustices effectively, considering the complex historical and societal influences shaping gay rights discourse.

Queering the Stage Beyond Russia: t.A.T.u. and Pussy Riots in a Global Political Context

While Alexander Wendt (1995) paved the way for constructivism in international relations theory after experts, scholars and pundits fell short to predict the fall of the Berlin Wall in 1989 and consequently the implosion of the Soviet Union. Cynthia Weber (2016) led the charge in view of providing a better understanding of queer politics in international relations. Her work deconstructs and reassesses notions of normalcy and perverseness against the backdrop of an empirical case study of Tom Neuwirth, better known as Conchita Wurst, a transgender Austrian music artist and drag queen, who won the Eurovision Song Contest in 2014 (Weber 2016, Chapters 2 and 6). Drawing on some of these earlier insights, we provide a short overview of the role of Russian performance and music artists that have shaped queer spaces in the context of national politics and fueled official, reactionary responses to their activities. Here, we focus on two primary examples, the Russian pop duo t.A.T.u., consisting of Lena Katina and Julia Volkova, and the Russian punk band, Pussy Riot, founded by Nadya Tolokonnikova and consisting of approximately eleven members.[1] The latter, however, is more than just a music group and could best be described as a group of Russian feminist and performance artists with a transnational reach and iconoclastic messaging (Bruce 2015).

Pussy Riot was created in 2011 and despite more recent performative and artistic engagements, it has incited greater public and scholarly debate than t.A.T.u., which has its roots in the late 1990s, representing Russia in the 2003 Eurovision competition (see for instance Riccioni and Halley 2021; Tuttle 2016; Wiedlack and Neufeld 2014). Notwithstanding, the pop duo represents an important juncture in Russia's cultural and political environment at the time. Both artists could be considered mainstream, with their producer and manager, Ivan Shapovalov, creating an iconic and globally selling product brand. Their lesbian performativity, kissing each other on stage in 2003, certainly drew the public eye and criticism from concerned parents, as the duo were minors. This includes their first big hit, the provocative song "All the things she said" which was released in 2002 (Heller 2017). Yet other songs, such as "Not Gonna Get Us," are less provocative and sexualized, thus creating "a symbolic juncture between the clusters of teenage angst, female bonding, intimacy, social pressure, female rebellion and pleasure (Bode and Tolstikova 2006, 126). The theatrical and at times juxtaposition of cultural tropes and imaginations that pit Western against Russian values are further highlighted by interviews given by the duo, including the music TV channel MTV, explaining that "Everybody thinks we are lesbians. But we just love each other" (Bode and Tolstikova 2006). Despite their solo careers during most of the 2010s—they were active between 1999–2011 and reunited post-pandemic in 2022 for some tours—they performed at the 2014 Sochi Winter Olympic games, a time of heightened gay rights repression (Clarke 2013). Their commodified appearances and their less provocative and protest-focused performances made them less of a trojan battlehorse for gay rights activists and were considered less of an ideological regime threat, stirring only minimal identity politics.

Pussy Riot, on the contrary, has struck a different chord in terms of musical performance, activism and their public engagement. Members of the band have been sentenced and imprisoned by Russian authorities and their vocal advocacy work, along with performance-driven activities have shaped a cultural weapon against Putin's regime. Their early global appearance with amateur-produced footage in Moscow's orthodox church, Christ the Savior Cathedral, went viral on social media in 2012 and demonstrates a raw and hands-on struggle for justice within a very repressive society (Datta-Paulin 2012). Since then, their activism and performances have turned into professional and highly curated, artistically provocative performative music videos—for a global distribution and audience to garner support—alongside their media appearances (interviews) and performance art (Pussy Riot 2013).[2] The trial against members of the band by Russian authorities in 2012 for hooliganism and religious hatred was deemed absurd and spilled much ink in the global human rights arena (see, for instance, Denber 2012; Lipman 2012). More importantly, however, it projects a new, more global image of President Putin on the world stage. As Gulnaz Sharafutdinova highlights, the Russian leader was able to promote a discourse in view of morality politics, conveying a conservative and traditional values-oriented image beyond his territorial borders. The domestically centered issue thus grew in transnational proportions (Sharafutdinova 2014). The discursive space occupied by official authorities thus competes with the artistic, affect-driven calls to support the Pussy Riot agenda in view of greater freedom based on gender issues and provocative, radical feminism.

Transitioning from the live performances and provocative acts of t.A.T.u. and Pussy Riot, we now turn our attention to a newer wave of queer expression in Russia that navigates the complex terrain of social media. The internet has emerged as a vital space for LGBTQ individuals and communities to articulate their identities, share experiences, and mobilize for rights within an increasingly restrictive sociopolitical climate. These digital arenas not only offer refuge and solidarity but also challenge the pervasive narratives enforced by the state and society. In the following section, we will delve into the impact of these online communities and the role they play in shaping contemporary queer activism in Russia.

The Legal Landscape and Online Spaces as Sites of Engagement

The "gay propaganda law" of 2013 marked a significant shift on the national scale, yet previous legislation targeting the freedom of expression of non-heterosexual Russians has existed since as early as 2006 at regional and local levels. These laws were adopted across ten cities and oblasts in

Russia, and the threat of imposition in St. Petersburg in 2011–2012 led to vigorous protests from the local queer community that drew international attention (Radzhana Buyantueva 2018). Nevertheless, the following year, the national law was implemented, as part of a national-ideological campaign to portray Russia as a defender of so-called "traditional values" challenging the dominance of the West. This campaign was closely linked to increasing assertiveness of foreign policy through the introduction of "sovereign democracy" and "democratic multipolarity," serving as a bulwark against perceived incursions through "color revolutions" across the former Soviet Bloc, NATO, and the EU (Radzhana Buyantueva 2018; Stepanova 2015; Wilkinson 2014).

This rise in officially promoted conservatism, closely connected with anti-Western rhetoric, and the subsequent increase in state repression against non-heterosexual Russians was also strengthened by a number of other interrelated factors, including the growing religiosity of Russians and the sociopolitical influence of the Russian Orthodox Church (Jarzyńska 2014), demographic concerns (Pecherskaya 2013), and democratic repression following the 2011–2012 popular protests "For Free and Fair Elections" headed by prominent members of the political opposition (Dmitriev 2015). Thus, as Buyantueva notes, anti-LGBTQ "rhetoric fit well in the state's conservative anti-Western discourse by presenting [LGBTQ] people as a negative Western influence and a threat to Russians' morality and traditional values," which in turn "vindicated" the increased state repression of non-heterosexual Russians (R. Buyantueva 2021).

While the "gay propaganda law" is the most famous legislation, other laws included the so-called "foreign agents law," which mandated the registration of NGOs as "foreign agents" if they receive foreign funding the introduction of criminal responsibility and tightening of punishments for organizing public protests; the banning of "unwelcome organizations" seen to threaten state security and the public; and the banning of the adoption of Russian children by same-sex couples and by foreigners from countries that had legalized same-sex marriage (R. Buyantueva 2021). This legislation, Cai Wilkinson (2014) argues, has furthered the state rhetoric of "traditional values" through the usage of homophobia as a foundation for the construction of Russian national identity as distinct from the West. Since the imposition of legislation targeted at "foreign agents," a banner or message highlighting how the material on any given website or even message through the popular social media service Telegram is "produced, distributed, and (or) sent by a foreign agent…or concerns the activities of a foreign agent" has been legally mandated,[3] which has assisted in the governmental delegitimization and ongoing dismantling of civil society in Russia.

Previously, Russian queer activists led a wide variety of cultural and educational events, petitioning, litigation, and public engagements ranging from film festivals to Pride marches. By the late 2010s, "growing political constraints complicated further development of [LGBTQ] activism forcing activists to adapt to the hostile political environment by changing their tactics and strategies" to reduce the risk of homophobic attacks and harassment, both from street threats and the police (R. Buyantueva 2021). The COVID-19 pandemic, full-scale invasion of Ukraine, and increased crackdowns, however, even further reduced the level of visibility of many Russian queer activist NGOs and public spaces. Though the late 2000s had seen the rise of multiple LGBTQ groups and organizations–including the first and only Russian interregional umbrella organization the Russian LGBT Network (*Rossiskaya LGBT Set'*), the Samara-based Avers, the Arkhangel'sk-based Rakurs, the Murmansk-based Maximum, the St. Petersburg-based Coming Out – the increased governmental repression, surveillance, and a November 2023 Supreme Court ruling designating the international LGBTQ movement as an "extremist organization" that incites "social and religious hatred" has even further restricted the level of activists' engagements (Ioanes 2023).

In this environment of [extreme repression], the internet and social media have come to play "a significant role not only by contributing to the development of [LGBTQ] communities in Russian cities, but also by helping to establish and maintain connections between [LGBTQ] rights activists"(R. Buyantueva 2021, 462). While in use as early as the late 1990s to spread awareness among the LGBTQ community—as in the case of the popular website Gay.ru, founded in 1997—the internet has become an increasingly essential resource as physical activities have become ever more restricted, used by formal civil society organizations (CSOs), activist networks, and individual initiatives alike. However, as the importance of the internet has grown over the past decade, so too have the repressive measures put in place by the Russian government—"virtual" persecution has largely been spearheaded by the Russian Federal Service for Supervision of Communications, Information, Technology, and Mass Media (Roskomnadzor), whose ongoing surveillance and "blacklists" have served to restrict even the online presence of many queer human rights organizations, as in the case of Gay.ru, blocked in Russia in 2018 for violation of the law against "propaganda of non-traditional sexual relations" (Ring 2018). Nevertheless, these queer "in-between spaces" have continued to proliferate online, overcoming strong governmental resistance to serve as a source of support and community for LGBTQ+ Russians.

Adapting to a Repressive Environment

Since the further restriction of the civil rights of non-heterosexual Russians in the early 2020s, much of the focus of CSOs has broadly centered on three pillars of support for the LGBTQ community, including legal and psychological aid and anti-discrimination monitoring. This restriction has similarly affected the level of available access to many Russian LGBTQ CSOs: the case of the Russian LGBT Network proves illustrative. In both the English and Russian language versions of the organizational website, the latest news update of 12 September 2023 is inaccessible, with only a donation link available on the English site and redirection to an administrator login on the Russian edition; furthermore, no other organization news is available. The social media pages of the Network have similarly been largely discontinued: the Vkontakte page is no longer available to the public and the organization's YouTube channel has had all content removed; the Network's X (Twitter) page, however, continues to share information on psychological and legal assistance in connection with the "gay propaganda laws" as of April 2023, on an informational campaign entitled "#We'reHere (*#MyTut*)" run by the Network, and on efforts by the state to shut down various LGBTQ+ rights organizations based in Russia, including the Sphere Foundation (*Fond Sphera*), and where to find further information, including through the creation of a "LGBT+ Help Bot" on the popular social media service Telegram, through which users can send requests for psychological and legal support. Despite the continuance of activities, however, there is noticeable decrease in the amount of posts between late 2020 to present day: posts from 2021 feature a vast range of activities, ranging from continual references to the psychological and legal support offered by the Network to webinars and lectures featuring politicians and academics, translations of LGBT family-oriented children's books, posts on days of queer visibility, circulation of petitions against the imposition of "anti-LGBT propaganda" laws, information on various government and legal actions related to LGBTQ+ websites and organizations, and profiles on specific individuals and their family who faced persecution at the governmental level, including through appeals to the European Court of Human Rights.

The case of the Sphere Foundation, another major LGBTQ human rights organization, provides an interesting comparison to the Russian LGBTQ Network. Founded in 2011 to "raise awareness and advocate for the Russian LGBT+ community through coordinated campaigns...provide direct assistance to LBT_ community members...[and] partner with other human rights organizations that share our goals," the Sphere Foundation divides its activities into two broad categories: "strategic programs," and "social help". The former focuses on human rights monitoring, advocacy work, so-called strategic litigation, and, most recently, a gender equality initiative. The latter includes psychological and legal assistance to support asylum-seeking cases outside the Russian Federation.[4] While the organization was officially disbanded by court order in April 2022, it continues its social and legal support initiatives, and maintains an active social media presence. The Sphere Foundation engages through Instagram, X (formerly Twitter), Telegram, Facebook and YouTube. These channels allow the organization to raise awareness about the ongoing persecution of LGBTQ human rights in Russia. They highlight profiles of individuals who fought for queer rights, share information on web-based Pride activities, like the 2024 "GenQ Pride Fest 'It Cannot Be Banned' (*Zapretit' nel'zya byt'*)," calls for creative works from queer Russians, organizational impact infographics, and monthly updates on "Good LGBT+ News."[5] Despite being officially banned, the organization reaches thousands of viewers, particularly on Telegram, with near-daily updates. The presumed target audience of their online advocacy varies by medium. For example, the Sphere Foundation's X page posts in both Russian and English, while their Instagram and Telegram posts are primarily in Russian. They also share information on other post-Soviet countries, such as a post from 17 May 2024, on the International Day of the Fight Against Queerphobia.

In addition to the prominent CSOs maintaining a presence on social media despite ongoing governmental repression, several newer initiatives have arisen since 2020. Typically less formal in nature, but still widespread across social media platforms, these initiatives have managed to build their audiences in a climate of repression, serving as "in-between" spaces to profile various resources and creative endeavors. "Kvir Media," one organization, is described as "queer media from queer people…[we] discuss life and problems of society through personal stories, scientific facts, discussions, news, and memes."[6] Founded in March 2023, the media organization is far more recent than the other organizations profiled but has built a comparable online following, with posts racking up hundreds to thousands of views. Rather than highlighting psychological or legal assistance, Kvir Media's daily posts instead feature articles on LGBT+ rights and visibility both within Russia and around the world, particularly in relation to trans- or non-binary gender identities, artworks celebrating queer days of visibility, particular artists, and even live-events, such as a queer stand-up comedy night held in Tbilisi, Georgia. Like the other LGBT+ rights organizations profiled, Kvir Media similarly utilizes multiple modes of social media, including an active presence on Teletype, Instagram, and Telegram, all linked through their home website.[7]

The online-based activism group "Snow Initiative (*SNeG*)," described as a "non-binary initiative…from non-binary people for non-binary people" according to its primary website was founded in November 2022 and is present on multiple platforms, including X, Instagram, and Telegram, and features many educational resources for neurodivergency in Russia, psychological consultations, a timeline of anti-Trans legislation in Russia, and other personal guides and services for their queer audience. "Gender Blender," another web-based queer initiative, also features multiple social media channels, including active Instagram and Telegram accounts, a blog on queer books, drag queens, and films, and the link to the organization's podcast, which ran for two seasons and, as of March 2023, was listed on Roskomnadzor's "Unified Registry of Domain Names Containing Information Prohibited for Distribution in the Russian Federation."[8] In addition to their own online resources, the initiative also features a link to another NGO, "Queer Svit," an organization centered around "helping LGBTQ+ and BIPOC who were affected by war [in Ukraine],"[9] and, like the Russian anti-war initiative "Kovcheg (The Ark),"[10] shares information designed to help those facing persecution in Russia, especially LGBTQ individuals, to emigrate from the country. All of these queer initiatives have been affected by the imposition of targeted anti-LGBTQ+ legislation, tightened internet controls linked to Russia's ongoing invasion of Ukraine, and individual criminal prosecutions on account of supposed violations of "terrorism" or queer extremism. While the initiatives described above continue to function—and a couple even originate during the post-2022 period—the scope of activities has been limited, ranging from services restricted to events canceled to websites added to Roskomnadzor's list of blocked domains to, in the case of the Sphere Foundation, a court-ordered liquidation in April 2022. Similarly, the civil society organizations described above have all been subject to the anti-"foreign agents" law, and all their websites, posts, and other methods of communication have been marked by banners declaring that their material was "produced, distributed, and (or) sent by a foreign agent." The imposition of the "foreign agents law," while not unique within the paradigm of civil society, aligns well with official state and state-sponsored rhetoric denouncing queerness as a foreign or Western import hostile to the "traditional values" paraded by the Putin regime as innate to Russia.

Conclusion

This chapter critically examined repressive political strategies used by autocratic regimes, particularly in Russia, to manage existential threats through scapegoating LGBTQ communities. By comparing Poland's political landscape, the chapter elucidated how ideological and historical contexts shape LGBTQ experiences and struggles. While Poland's shift towards a pro-EU coalition offers potential for queer rights, cultural and religious conservatism poses significant challenges. Conversely, entrenched heteropatriarchal nationalism under Putin exacerbates LGBTQ persecution in Russia, pushing queer activism underground.

The chapter contrasted the impacts of political changes on LGBTQ rights in Poland and Russia, highlighting how each country's socio-political dynamics influence repression. Poland's resistance to LGBTQ rights is driven by religious conservatism and the Catholic Church, hindering consistent implementation of anti-discrimination policies despite EU mandates. In Russia, the Soviet legacy of criminalizing non-heteronormative identities persists, with Putin's regime reinforcing traditional values and increasing discrimination through measures like the 2013 "gay propaganda" law. Russian queer activism, using social media campaigns and educational initiatives, shows resilience despite severe repression.

The chapter also examined Russia's antagonism towards Western values, influencing its repressive policies, and contrasted this with Poland's EU-driven opportunities and constraints for LGBTQ advocacy. The historical context of queerness in Russia, cultural figures like t.A.T.u. and Pussy Riot, and the shift in activism to virtual spaces were discussed.

Transitioning to our next chapter, we will explore a meta-analysis of collective action and contentious politics in various regions. This final chapter will present a framework for understanding LGBTQ struggles in diverse settings, providing a tool to map and analyze LGBTQ advocacy challenges and strategies. Our reflections will underscore the importance of a cross-disciplinary, intersectional approach in furthering research and understanding critical issues. This geo-mapping and data visualization analysis will offer insights into LGBTQ activism's resilience and adaptability, inspiring continued efforts toward equality and justice.

Notes

1 Current members include Nadya Tolokonnikova, Yekaterina Samutsevich, Taisiya Krugovykh, Vasily Bogatov, Diana Burkot, Maria Alyokhina, Lusine Dzhanyan, Alexey Knedlyakovsky, Rita Flores, Veronika Nikulshina, Olga Kurachyova, Olga Pakhtusova, Olga Borisova, Alexander Sofeyev, and Lucy Shtein.
2 See also artist website at https://pussyriot.love/, accessed 23 June 2024.
3 Russian LGBT Network, home page, https://lgbtnet.org/en/
4 Sphere Foundation, "About Us," https://spherequeer.org/en/about/.
5 Instagram account: https://www.instagram.com/spherequeer/, and Telegram: https://t.me/s/spherequeer, accessed 30 July 2024.
6 Kvir Media X page, https://x.com/kvir_media, accessed 30 July 2024.
7 Kvir Media home page, https://taplink.cc/kvir.media, accessed 30 July 2024.
8 As shared on the Gender Blender Instagram account: https://www.instagram.com/genderblender3000/p/CqSN0MkrnZO/, accessed 30 July 2024
9 "Queer Svit" Instagram page, available at: https://www.instagram.com/queer_svit/, accessed 30 July 2024.
10 See The Ark Project (Project Kovcheg) for more information: https://kovcheg.live/about/, accessed 30 July 2024.

References

Afshar, Ahoura. 2006. "The Anti-Gay Rights Movement in the United States: The Framing of Religion." *Essex Human Rights Review* 3 (1): 64–79.
Baer, Brian James. 2016. "Queer in Russia: Othering the Other of the West." In *Queer in Europe*, 173–88. Abingdon: Routledge.
Bode, Matthias, and N. Tolstikova. 2006. "Kissing to Be Clever: Gender Politics of Pop, the Russian Way." *GCB - Gender and Consumer Behavior Volume* 8: 117–33.
Bruce, Caitlin. 2015. "The Balaclava as Affect Generator: Free Pussy Riot Protests and Transnational Iconicity." *Communication and Critical/Cultural Studies* 12 (1): 42–62.
Buyantueva, R. 2021. "LGBT Russians and Political Environment for Activism." *Communist and Post-Communist Studies* 54 (3): 119–36.
Buyantueva, Radzhana. 2018. "LGBT Rights Activism and Homophobia in Russia." *Journal of Homosexuality* 65 (4): 456–83.

Clarke, Liz. 2013. "Russia's Anti-Gay Law Brings Controversy ahead of 2014 Sochi Olympics." *The Washington Post*, August 18, 2013. https://www.washingtonpost. com/sports/olympics/russias-anti-gay-law-brings-controversy-ahead-of-2014-sochi-olympics/2013/08/18/b42b5182-076f-11e3-9259-e2aafe5a5f84_story.html

Datta-Paulin, Sam. 2012. *Pussy Riot: Scuffles Outside Court Hearing of Russian Punk Band Who Raided Moscow Cathedral*. Youtube. https://www.youtube.com/ watch?v=P3cLEv402Hg.

Davydova, D. 2019. "Between Heteropatriarchy and Homonationalism: Codes of Gender, Sexuality, and Race/ethnicity in Putin's Russia," November. https://yorkspace. library.yorku.ca/items/4db5fcf8-80d7-4396-b2fc-ed977343d2a4.

Denber, Rachel. 2012. "Pussy Riot and Russia's Surreal 'Justice.'" Human Rights Watch. August 17, 2012. https://www.hrw.org/news/2012/08/17/pussy-riot-and-russias-surreal-justice.

Dmitriev, Mikhail. 2015. "Lost in Transition? The Geography of Protests and Attitude Change in Russia." *Europe-Asia Studies* 67 (2): 224–43.

Eigenmann, L. 2022. "'This Is a Union of Values': The Rise of the LGBTI Rights Norm as Part of the EU's Identity Construction." *Social Politics: International Studies in Gender*. https://academic.oup.com/sp/article-abstract/29/1/95/6358602

Essig, Laurie. 1999. *Queer in Russia: A Story of Sex, Self, and the Other*. Durham: Duke University Press.

Heller, D. 2017. "'Russian Body and Soul': tATu Performs at Eurovision 2003." *A Song for Europe*. https://doi.org/10.4324/9781315097732-10/russian-body-soul-performs-eurovision-2003-dana-heller

Ioanes, Ellen. 2023. "Russia's Absurd Claim That the LGBTQ Community Is Extremist, Explained." Vox. December 5, 2023. https://www.vox.com/world-politics/ 2023/12/5/23988527/russia-anti-lgbtq-ruling-extremist-putin

Jarzyńska, Katarzyna. 2014. "The Russian Orthodox Church as Part of the State and Society." *Russian Politics & Law* 52 (3): 878–97.

Kerf, Justine De. 2017. "Anti-Gay Propaganda Laws: Time for the European Court of Human Rights to Overcome Her Fear of Commitment." *DiGeSt Journal of Diversity and Gender Studies* 4 (1): 35.

Levitanus, Mariya, and Polina Kislitsyna. 2024. "'Why Wave the Flag?': (in)visible Queer Activism in Authoritarian Kazakhstan and Russia." *Central Asian Survey* 43 (1): 12–32.

Lipman, Masha. 2012. "The Absurd and Outrageous Trial of Pussy Riot." *The New Yorker*, August 7, 2012. https://www.newyorker.com/news/news-desk/the-absurd-and-outrageous-trial-of-pussy-riot

Mitchell, T. 2016. "Queer Identity and Socialist Realism: The Censorship of Queer Art and Life under Stalin and beyond," April. https://deepblue.lib.umich.edu/bitstream/ handle/2027.42/120609/tgmitch.pdf?isAllowe

Mole, Richard C. M., ed. 2020. *Soviet and Post-Soviet Sexualities*. London, England: Routledge. https://doi.org/10.4324/9781315623078

Pecherskaya, N. V. 2013. "Perspektivy Rossiiskoi Semejnoi Politiki: Prinuzhdenie K Traditsii [Prospects for Russian Family Policy: The Drive towards Tradition]." *Zhurnal Sotsiologii I Sotsialnoi Antropologii* 69 (4): 94–105.

Pussy Riot. 2013. Youtube. https://www.youtube.com/channel/UCQYcCfKYfYMcu Csem8z5CyQ

Ramet, Sabrina P. 2019. *Orthodox Churches and Politics in Southeastern Europe*. Cham: Springer International Publishing.

Riccioni, Ilaria, and Jeffrey A. Halley. 2021. "Performance as Social Resistance: Pussy Riot as a Feminist Avant-Garde." *Theory, Culture & Society* 38 (7–8): 211–31.

Ring, Trudy. 2018. "LGBT Website Gay.ru Blocked Within Russia." Advocate.com. April 2, 2018. https://www.advocate.com/world/2018/4/02/lgbt-website-gayru-blocked-within-russia.

Rivkin-Fish, Michele, and Cassandra Hartblay. 2014. "When Global LGBTQ Advocacy Became Entangled with New Cold War Sentiment: A Call for Examining Russian Queer Experience." *The Brown Journal of World Affairs* 21 (1): 95–111.

Sharafutdinova, Gulnaz. 2014. "The Pussy Riot Affair and Putin's Démarche from Sovereign Democracy to Sovereign Morality." *Nationalities Papers* 42 (4): 615–21.

Siegel, Scott N. 2020. "Rainbows and Crosses: Noncompliance with EU Law Prohibiting Sexual Orientation Discrimination." *Journal of European Social Policy* 30 (2): 241–58.

Stepanova, Elena. 2015. "'the Spiritual and Moral Foundation of Civilization in Every Nation for Thousands of Years': The Traditional Values Discourse in Russia." *Politics Religion & Ideology* 16 (2-3): 119–36.

Suchland, Jennifer. 2018. "The LGBT Specter in Russia: Refusing Queerness, Claiming 'Whiteness.'" *Gender, Place and Culture: A Journal of Feminist Geography* 25 (7): 1073–88.

Tuttle, Tara. 2016. "Deranged Vaginas: Pussy Riot's Feminist Hermeneutics." *The Journal of Religion and Popular Culture* 28 (2-3): 67–80.

Weber, Cynthia. 2016. *Queer International Relations. Oxford Studies in Gender and International Relations*. New York: Oxford University Press.

Wendt, Alexander. 1995. "Constructing International Politics." *International Security* 20 (1): 71–81.

Wiedlack, Katharina, and Masha Neufeld. 2014. "Lost in Translation? Pussy Riot Solidarity Activism and the Danger of Perpetuating North/Western Hegemonies." *Religion and Gender* 4 (2): 145–65.

Wilkinson, Cai. 2014. "Putting 'traditional Values' into Practice: The Rise and Contestation of Anti-Homopropaganda Laws in Russia." *Journal of Human Rights* 13 (3): 363–79.

Zhabenko, Alisa. 2019. "Russian Lesbian Mothers: Between 'traditional Values' and Human Rights." *Journal of Lesbian Studies* 23 (3): 321–35.

Part 3

Queer Topography

The final section reaches its peak in Chapter 8, presenting a comprehensive meta-analysis of the issues at hand and offering a broad perspective on various collective actions and contentious politics. This chapter details a range of subversive activities within oppressive sociopolitical and cultural environments, enriching the conceptual framework established at the beginning of our book to enhance the understanding of the daily challenges faced by LGBTQ communities across different regions. Our conclusion weaves together the book's central themes, contemplating the wider implications of our research. The authors highlight the interconnected nature of LGBTQ struggles with global sociopolitical and ecological changes, providing valuable insights for future research and advocacy efforts.

DOI: 10.4324/9781003565871-11

8   A Cartography of Stakeholders and Subversive Activities

Building upon the critical examination of repressive political strategies outlined in previous chapters, this chapter's meta-analysis aims to synthesize and expand upon the insights gained from various case studies. The previous chapters' foci on the contrasting experiences of LGBTQ populations in Russia and Poland highlighted the complex interplay between political, cultural, and historical factors in shaping queer rights and activism. This chapter will extend this analysis, drawing on data visualization tools that not only contextualizes these struggles but also provides valuable tools for future research and advocacy. By showcasing a variety of activities that could primarily be defined as subversive given the often repressive sociopolitical and cultural backdrop of where LGBTQ advocates and community members engage, the authors complement the conceptual framework introduced at the beginning of our book and build on a number of case studies to better map and understand the daily struggles faced by members of the LGBTQ community across different regions and contexts.

Tying back into our discussion we initiated in Chapter 2 of this book, particularly on the historical overview of mapping and visualization of challenging contexts and conditions, we lay out several projects that have engaged with tracing and tracking queer voices online. As our case studies dealt with repressive and oftentimes hostile environments for sexual minorities, suffice it to say that the objective in this section does not lie in creating a traceable record of these (in)visible and (in)audible individuals and groups and unnecessarily endanger their lives and livelihoods. Yet these primarily North American examples illustrate how foundational knowledge sets the stage for exploring the advancements in geo-mapping software, like ArcGIS, and other visualization tools that have revolutionized how we document and analyze LGBTQ experiences. These technologies enable the creation of interactive maps that illustrate the spatial dimensions of queer life, offering new insights into how geographical and sociopolitical contexts influence LGBTQ activism and community building. In the methods section that follows, we detail the data and resources utilized in this meta-analysis, drawing from a diverse array of case studies to construct a comprehensive typology of subversive activities. These activities, often occurring in repressive environments, demonstrate the

DOI: 10.4324/9781003565871-12

innovative and adaptive strategies employed by LGBTQ advocates to navigate and challenge systemic oppression. By examining these case studies, we aim to identify common patterns and unique approaches that highlight the resilience and ingenuity of queer communities.

As mentioned in Chapter 2, a significant portion of this chapter is dedicated to the meta-analysis of case studies from various regions, drawing on public data sets, geo maps, and our empirical research using various data visualization tools. For instance, we explore the longitudinal analysis of public opinion and legal changes over time in countries like within the MENA region, Singapore and Russia. These visualizations provide a dynamic view of how LGBTQ rights and perceptions evolve, offering a deeper understanding of the sociopolitical forces at play. In the MENA region, we analyze the impact of geopolitical tensions and cultural conservatism on LGBTQ rights, highlighting both the challenges and the pockets of resistance that emerge in such contexts. Similarly, in Singapore, we examine the gradual shifts in public opinion towards greater acceptance of LGBTQ individuals, despite the persistence of conservative legal frameworks. By mapping these changes, we can better understand the interplay between grassroots advocacy and institutional reform. Russia presents a particularly stark case, where the legacy of Soviet-era repression and the current regime's nationalist agenda create a hostile environment for LGBTQ activism. Our analysis includes a longitudinal study of public opinion, legal measures, and the covert strategies adopted by activists to sustain their efforts in the face of severe repression. These maps and visualizations serve as powerful tools for illustrating the nuanced and often perilous landscape navigated by queer communities. The findings and discussions generated from these maps and case studies culminate in a broader understanding of different LGBTQ movements across varying contexts. By presenting a typology of subversive activities and strategies, this chapter provides researchers, advocates, and students with a guiding framework for analyzing and supporting LGBTQ activism across different regions. The cross-disciplinary and intersectional approach underscores the interconnectedness of these struggles, emphasizing the need for a holistic perspective in both research and practice. In conclusion, Chapter 8 aims to inspire further research and advocacy by offering a comprehensive and nuanced analysis of LGBTQ activism in various sociopolitical contexts. By leveraging the power of geo-mapping and data visualization, we hope to shed light on the resilience and adaptability of queer communities, ultimately contributing to the ongoing fight for equality and justice.

Global North Queer Geo Mapping Projects vs. LGBTQ Invisibility in Repressive Contexts

Geo-mapping projects dedicated to the LGBTQ community play a crucial role in documenting, preserving, and sharing queer histories, experiences, and spaces across the globe. These digital initiatives create interactive maps that

highlight significant locations related to LGBTQ life, offering both a historical record and a contemporary guide for queer individuals. As a case in point,
Queering the Map is a community-driven project where users contribute their
own stories and experiences connected to specific geographical locations
worldwide. This platform allows LGBTQ individuals to share personal narratives, fostering a sense of global solidarity and visibility.[1] Another project led
by municipal efforts, *The NYC LGBT Historic Sites Project*, focuses on New
York City, mapping sites of historical and cultural significance to the LGBTQ
community. The initiative highlights landmarks, such as Stonewall Inn, that
have played pivotal roles in the fight for LGBTQ rights. By showcasing these
locations, the project helps educate a broad public about the rich queer history embedded within the city.[2] Academics, such as researchers at Washington
University in St. Louis, have also engaged in recording local queer history. In
a project called *Mapping LGBTQ St. Louis*, the creators document the city's
LGBTQ history through an interactive map. It includes stories and data points
about significant locations, offering a localized yet comprehensive view of the
community's evolution and struggles, hosted online by the university library.[3]
It uses ArcGIS StoryMaps as the software platform to present the various
locations and narratives. In a similar vein, *Queer Sacramento* provides an
interactive map of historical and current LGBTQ places and events of Califor-
nia's capital. The project emphasizes local queer history, connecting past and
present through geolocated stories and information.[4] Two more projects are
noteworthy here. First, *Mapping the Gay Guides*, which maps the locations
listed in Bob Damron's Address Books, travel guides for gay men published
from the 1960s to the 2000s. It offers a unique historical perspective on the
evolution of gay travel and social spaces over several decades, highlighting
changes in societal attitudes and the resilience of the LGBTQ community.[5]
And second, *OutHistory*, though not exclusively a mapping project, it includes maps and geolocated stories as part of its broader mission to document
LGBTQ history. The platform provides a diverse array of historical accounts,
making queer history accessible and engaging.[6]

   Despite the success and importance of these projects in many parts of the
world, similar tools are conspicuously absent in authoritative-leaning countries, such as Russia and many Arab nations. The primary reason for this absence is the severe repression of sexual minorities in these regions. LGBTQ
individuals face significant legal and social challenges, including criminali-
zation, discrimination, and violence, making the development and deployment of such geo-mapping tools extremely risky. In Russia, for example,
the government has implemented anti-LGBTQ laws, such as the 2013 "gay
propaganda" law, which prohibits the promotion of non-traditional sexual
relationships with minors. This legislation has been used to justify censorship and repression, effectively stifling LGBTQ activism and visibility. Any
attempt to create a public, interactive map documenting queer experiences
would likely be met with severe backlash, including legal repercussions for

the creators and contributors. Similarly, in many Arab countries, homosexuality is criminalized, and LGBTQ individuals face severe penalties, including imprisonment, corporal punishment, and even death. The societal stigma and legal repercussions associated with being openly LGBTQ make it nearly impossible to safely develop and share geo-mapping tools. Activists in these regions often work under pseudonyms and use secure, discreet methods to connect and share information, but the fear of exposure and retribution remains a significant barrier. The absence of LGBTQ geo-mapping projects in these regions underscores the critical need for continued global advocacy for LGBTQ rights. While technology has the power to connect and empower marginalized communities, the political and social environment must also be conducive to such initiatives. Until there is a broader acceptance and protection of LGBTQ rights in authoritative-leaning countries, the potential of geo-mapping tools to document and celebrate queer lives will remain unrealized in these areas.

Methodological Considerations

Before delving into our data analysis, we outline our methodological choices for examining our social media content from different geographic locations. To capture a comprehensive view of LGBTQ community experiences and activism across varying regions, we utilized web scraping techniques and the software tool Octoparse[7] to gather data from platform X. This methodology involved several key steps. First, we configured Octoparse to extract relevant data from the platform, focusing on posts, comments, and interactions that explicitly referenced LGBTQ issues, events, and movements. The scraping process was tailored to collect data from specific regional areas, including the MENA region, Singapore, and Russia, to capture diverse perspectives. We specifically targeted hashtags commonly associated with the LGBTQ community, such as #LGBTQ. To protect the privacy of our research subjects, we refrain from disclosing specific hashtag combinations used for data collection. Moreover, we employed Octoparse's advanced features, such as XPath and regular expressions, to refine data extraction and ensure the relevance of the collected information. Data was organized and categorized based on themes of advocacy, activism, and subversive activities. Following data extraction, we conducted a comparative analysis to identify patterns and trends in LGBTQ engagement across different regions using the text analysis software Voyant Tools.[8]

Voyant Tools is a web-based text analysis and visualization tool designed to help users explore and interpret large amounts of text data. It offers features for analyzing textual content, including word clouds, frequency lists, topic modeling, and trends and patterns analysis. As such, it is a versatile tool for understanding textual data and exploring how different texts relate to one another, helping us gain insights into the content through visual and interactive means. Our analysis was supported by qualitative coding and thematic analysis to uncover insights into the nature and scope of LGBTQ activism and subversion. Consequently, the findings contribute to a nuanced understanding of how LGBTQ communities navigate and influence social media landscapes in varying political and cultural contexts.

Data Processing, Cleaning, and Analysis

Once the data was collected, we proceeded with cleaning it to ensure accuracy and relevance, involving the removal of duplicates, filtering out non-relevant content, and standardizing data formats, such as dates or tweet counts. Our analysis was structured around three main themes: subversive activities, daily challenges, and advocacy work. Each theme was examined through the lens of the collected social media data, focusing on:

- **Subversive Activities:** Identifying and categorizing forms of resistance and defiance against oppressive structures, including underground movements and coded language used to avoid censorship.
- **Daily Challenges:** Highlighting the everyday struggles faced by LGBTQ individuals, such as discrimination, violence, and social exclusion.
- **Advocacy Work:** Documenting the efforts of activists and organizations in promoting LGBTQ rights, raising awareness, and providing support to community members.

As discussed in our conceptual framework in Chapter 1, our study recognizes the importance of intersectionality in understanding LGBTQ experiences. We paid particular attention to how various social identities, such as gender, race, class, and religion, intersect and influence the experiences of LGBTQ individuals in different regions. This intersectional perspective is crucial for a nuanced understanding of the unique challenges and forms of resilience within these communities. Additionally, our approach is inherently cross-disciplinary, drawing on methods and theories from sociology, digital humanities, queer studies, and data science. This fusion of disciplines allows for a more holistic understanding of the data and its implications.

Finally, given the sensitive nature of LGBTQ issues, especially in repressive environments, we ensured that our data collection and analysis adhered to strict ethical guidelines. We anonymized all personal identifiers to protect individuals' privacy and followed ethical standards for web scraping, including respecting the terms of service of the platforms used and obtaining necessary permissions when required. By leveraging social media data, this section provides a rich, detailed account of the LGBTQ community's struggles, resilience, and advocacy across the MENA region, Russia, and Singapore. Our findings offer a valuable resource for further research and advocacy, encouraging a deeper, more intersectional exploration of LGBTQ issues globally.

Visualization and Mapping Select Cases

In this section of our chapter, we turn to exploring some of the daily struggles of the LGBTQ community in select cases across the MENA region, Singapore and Russia. Instead of proposing a cookie-cutter approach, we draw on online data analysis through web scraping to highlight specific subversive activities, challenges and advocacy work across the social media platform X. These findings should serve as a framing tool for researchers, scholars, advocates, practitioners, and students. It aims to inspire further research through a cross-disciplinary, intersectional lens, fostering a deeper understanding of these critical issues.

Mixed Experiences Across the MENA Region

To help contextualize our regional social media analysis of countries situated across the Middle East and North Africa region we draw from public opinion surveys available on the public Equaldex website, a platform that tracks LGBTQ rights and public opinion globally.[9] Rather than limiting ourselves to the annual snapshot of public perceptions on the issue, we conducted a longitudinal analysis of public opinion on LGBTQ rights. It should be noted that Equaldex's Equality Index combines legal status and public attitudes to provide a comprehensive overview of LGBTQ issues across different countries.

Varying Public Opinion Trends on LGBTQ Rights in the MENA Region

When exploring public opinion in the region, some shifts over the years are noticeable, though it remains largely conservative compared to other regions. According to the website, countries like Jordan, Saudi Arabia, and the United Arab Emirates have low public opinion indices, indicating limited acceptance and support for LGBTQ individuals. For example, Jordan's public opinion index is at 6/100, while the UAE stands slightly higher at 25/100.[10] The disparity between legal rights and public opinion is also notable. In some MENA countries, legal frameworks are slowly evolving, but public opinion remains resistant. For instance, while Jordan has a higher legal index of 41/100[11] compared to Saudi Arabia's 7/100,[12] public opinion in both countries remains low, reflecting deep-seated cultural and social resistance. Within the MENA region, there are significant differences in public opinion. In more progressive areas like Lebanon, there is a slightly higher acceptance of LGBTQ rights compared to more conservative countries like Saudi Arabia or Iran. This variation is influenced by cultural, religious, and political factors specific to each country. It is worthwhile to mention here that the historical data available on Equaldex reveals that changes in public opinion are gradual. The overall trend shows a slight increase in acceptance, particularly among younger populations and in more urbanized areas. However, the pace of change is slow, and significant legal and societal barriers remain. The longitudinal data from Equaldex highlights the complexity of LGBTQ rights in the MENA region. While there are some positive trends, widespread acceptance and equal rights are far from being realized. Continuous monitoring and advocacy are essential to drive further progress in both legal reforms and public opinion.[13]

Resilience, Subversive Activities, and the Role of Social Media

In the MENA region, LGBTQ subversive activities are essential for resisting oppression and advocating for rights in an often-hostile environment. Online activism plays a significant role, with anonymous social media campaigns and encrypted messaging apps like Telegram and Signal providing secure communication channels. Underground support networks, including secret meetings and safe houses, offer refuge and support to those in immediate danger. Cultural subversion through art, literature, fashion, and drag performances challenges societal norms and censorship. As discussed in Chapter 4, organizations like Helem in Lebanon and Shams in Tunisia advocate for LGBTQ rights, often working in secrecy or facing significant challenges. Digital subversion includes online publications and virtual events, enabling community connection and organization without physical risk. Examples of these efforts include Helem's advocacy in Lebanon, LGBTQ individuals in Egypt using social media despite severe crackdowns, and Shams' public operations in Tunisia. These activities highlight the resilience and creativity of LGBTQ individuals and activists in navigating oppressive environments to fight for their rights and build supportive communities.

The analysis of tweet frequencies and content from the MENA dataset reveals significant insights into discussions around gender equality and LGBTQ issues. However, it's important to note that the scope of this analysis is constrained by the limitations imposed by the API restrictions on X (formerly Twitter). These restrictions limit the volume and types of data that can be accessed, which means that the dataset may not capture the full spectrum of conversations occurring on the platform. As a result, certain tweets, particularly those with fewer engagements or from less prominent accounts, might be underrepresented. Furthermore, the inability to access comprehensive tweet views restricts our understanding of the broader audience reach and impact of specific tweets. Despite these limitations, the available data provides valuable glimpses into the key themes and engagement patterns within the MENA region's discussions on gender equality and LGBTQ issues. Nonetheless, for a more holistic understanding, future research would benefit from more extensive access to platform data, enabling a deeper and more nuanced analysis.

The analysis of tweet frequencies over time shows periodic peaks, reflecting events or heightened discussions. Keywords like gender equality

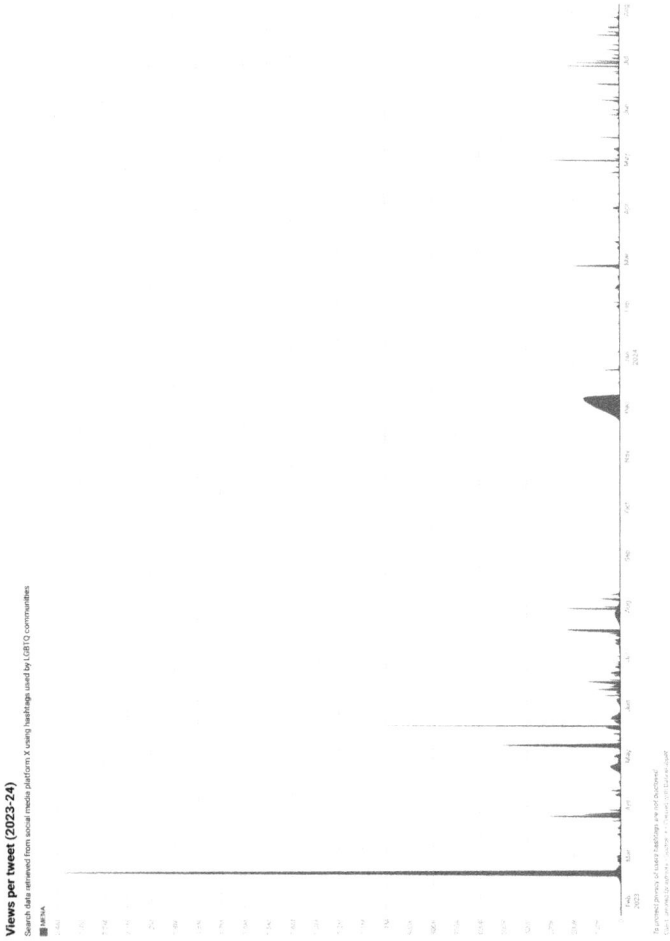

Graph 8.1 Chart with data on tweet views in the MENA region.

dominate the discourse, and tweets with high engagement metrics indicate the importance of these topics to the audience. We captured the tweet frequencies for the period between 2023 and 2024 (see Graph 8.2). The most visible peak in the graph with over 2.4 million views, for instance, was a post regarding the soccer club FC Barcelona standing in support of LGBTQ rights, tweeting to the Arab world and its fans on the International Day Against LGBT Hate in Sport in early 2023 (Graph 8.1).

Turning to word frequencies of the data set collected on the MENA, the analysis of tweet content reveals that discussions around LGBTQ issues within the dataset are heavily centered on community and gender identity, with "community" being the most frequently mentioned term. The graph shows significant relative frequencies for "community" in multiple segments, highlighting the focus on collective solidarity within LGBTQ discourse (Graph 8.2). The segments created with Voyant Tools refer to the timeline tweets that were posted during the period of 2023–2024. Discussions on "gender" also feature prominently, underscoring ongoing dialogues about gender equality and

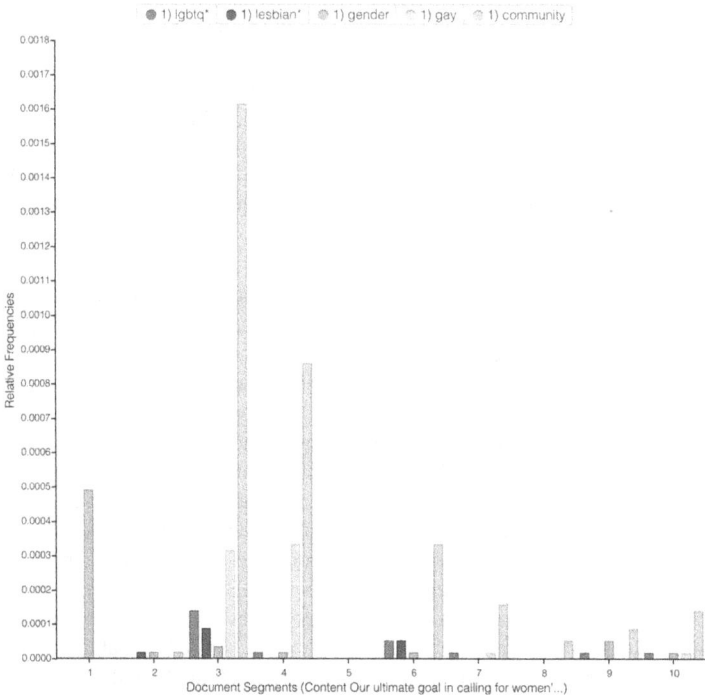

Graph 8.2 Chart with tweet data word frequencies between 2023 and 2024 in MENA region.

identity. Specific terms like "gay" and "lesbian" appear less frequently but are still significant, indicating focused attention on these identities. In contrast, broader terms like "lgbtq*" are mentioned less often, suggesting a preference for more specific terms within the community. These findings suggest that the discourse is nuanced, with a strong emphasis on solidarity and specific identity issues, guiding future advocacy and research efforts toward these focal points.

In the following, we take a closer look at social tensions and diverging perceptions of queer issues in Singapore.

Generational Divides and Growing Visibility in Singapore

As seen in our interviews with local activists in Singapore, public perception of the LGBTQ community and related queer rights issues has shifted noticeably over the previous years. Despite conservative opposition and a slow-moving state apparatus that remains wary of rapid change, younger demographics have been increasingly progressive-minded. Looking at data from Equaldex, we can see that general opinions on inclusive LGBTQ policies (such as same-sex marriage, greater LGBTQ rights, non-binary identifiers on official documentation etc.) are trending in favor of support rather than opposing these initiatives.[14] Certain issues that were clearly negatively viewed have also been trending in a favorable direction—take, for instance, "acceptance of homosexuals as neighbors." This particular topic featured a 31.64% "opposed" and a 68.31% "support" split in 2014. In 2022, the opposition would decrease to 25.65%, while support increased to 74.35%. A more recent example would be "support for same-sex couples' parenting." In 2020, opinion polls showed 39.2% opposed, with 28% supporting. However, by 2024, opposition had decreased to 29% and support increased to 56%.

Further examination of opinion research from other sources supports these insights. Ipsos' 2024 Pride study was "conducted across 26 countries including 500 respondents aged 21–74 in Singapore, [and] highlight[ed] a strong trend of growing support for LGBTQ+ rights in Singapore, particularly among Gen Z and Millenials" (Ho 2024) In their earlier 2023 study, it demonstrated a clear generational divide across issues related to queer individuals. Respondents belonging to Gen X (1965–1980) and Boomers (1948–1964) were consistently less supportive of the following: same-sex marriage, the right to adopt, and same-sex parenting. Interestingly, Ipsos' data also noted that women in Singapore were more likely to be supportive regarding these issues, highlighting further hierarchies that exist when examining how LGBTQ topics are perceived.

The importance of the annual Pink Dot event has been noted in Chapter 5, where a deliberately non-confrontational ethos has allowed for public expression of queer allyship to flourish. From its inception in 2009, the event has been held in the summer months and its impact is clear. Our social media scraping with Octoparse illustrates how online engagement increases around the time of this event (Graph 8.3).

Views per tweet (2023-24)

Search data retrieved from social media platform X using hashtags used by LGBTQ communities

Singapore

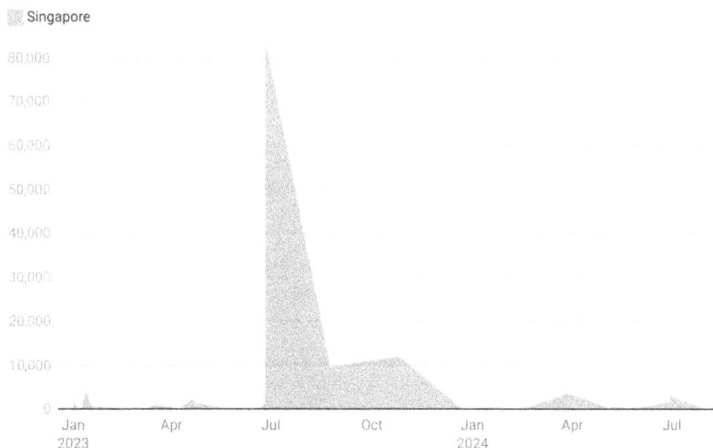

To protect privacy of users hashtags are not disclosed.

Chart created by the authors • Source: X • Created with Datawrapper

Graph 8.3 Chart with data on tweet views in Singapore.

The Pink Dot parade has therefore acted not only as a physical demonstration of solidarity, but also as a virtual rallying point via hashtags and online posts that maintain public awareness of the challenges faced by queer Singaporeans. Thus, its true impact is twofold, managing to spur discussion in both physical and online spaces every year. In a state where public activism is still viewed as being diametrically opposed to the deeply entrenched emphasis on social harmony, Pink Dot has been a valuable means by which a national conversation on LGBTQ rights can be maintained without overtly threatening the state's control. Its annual nature allows for activists and supporters to consistently coalesce—a matter that otherwise would be far trickier given the practical difficulties of political organization as well as the societal stigmas attached to such efforts.

Our data also showcases that most posts regarding Pink Dot maintain its non-confrontational spirit–statements mostly emphasize equality and integration, emphasizing a right to exist and thrive as any other Singaporean. As a result, these posts clearly outline the daily challenges faced by queer individuals, revealing nuances that might otherwise largely go unnoticed by the heteronormative public. Even if such statements are not directly subversive nor aiming to aggressively challenge opposing beliefs, their value lies in normalizing this debate and appealing to undecided bystanders. It is also helpful to realize that a movement of this size also allows for individuals in a conservative society to feel more emboldened to speak about their experiences, through the increased visibility of queer and straight allies that otherwise would be obscured due to state/societal censorship. Through our prior examination of Singapore's queer rights context, it is clear that this strategy is uniquely suited for the state, and the growing trend of support among the younger demographic is an optimistic signal for greater inclusivity moving forward. Next, we turn to our content analysis in the Russian-speaking X space.

Censorship Muting LGBTQ Visibility in Russia

The public opinion of LGBTQ rights within Russia has broadly worsened over the past thirty years, and significantly within the past decade. This fall is accompanied by a rise in negative media coverage and increasingly strident anti-LGBTQ rhetoric, couched within a broader trend of a return to traditional values set up in opposition to the West, and stringent legislation restricting the civil rights of LGBTQ individuals. As noted on the Equaldex site, Russia's equality index is now at a dismal 15/100, or 166th place in the world equality scale.[15] While both legal equality and public opinion are largely unfavorable, there remains a stark gap between the two frameworks. Legal equality is rated at 7/100, due not only to the well-known 2013 law banning "propaganda of non-traditional sexual relations," but also to a rash of more recent legislation, including the 2020 constitutional enshrinement of marriage as a union between a man and a woman, the November 2023 further restriction of so-called "LGBT propaganda" and "demonstration" of LGBT behavior, and the July 2023 ban on gender-affirming medical care and legal name change.[16] Public opinion remains low (22/100) due to strong social conservatism propagated by the regime, but fares better than the legal framework indicator. Focusing on the overall level of experienced equality, we notice that they differ across the vastness of the country. Although homosexuality has been federally decriminalized since 1993, it was re-instituted as a crime in Chechnya in 1996 during the region's de facto independence, and has since [served as a justification for multiple waves of horrific human rights abuses by Chechen police.[17] Non-heterosexual Russians across the country remain the target of extreme violence based on their sexuality and gender presentation, in increasing numbers since the furthering of anti-LGBTQ legislation over the past decade.[18] In contrast to the other regions surveyed within this book, social acceptance of LGBTQ persons has actually decreased significantly over the past twenty years, and as the Putin regime continues to hold onto power, this trend will likely continue.

Social Media (In)visibility and Activist Resilience

Since the proliferation of federal legislation targeting the LGBTQ community beginning in 2013 and a build-up of regime-guided negative public sentiment, heightened by laws targeting so-called 'foreign agents,' LGBTQ 'propaganda,' gender-affirming care, and the November 2023 declaration of the "international LGBTQ movement" as 'extremist,' non-heterosexual Russians have faced a systemic erosion of their rights within society. Furthermore, this persecution has not been limited solely to the 'physical' realm–the Russian Federal Service for Supervision of Communications, Information Technology, and Mass Media (Roskomnadzor)'s ongoing surveillance and 'blacklists' serve to restrict even the virtual presence of queer human-rights organizations. Nevertheless, queer 'in-between spaces' have continued to proliferate online, overcoming strong governmental resistance to serve as a source of support and community for LGBTQ+ persons. Given the severe legal and social restrictions present within Russia, many in-person gathering spaces face significant challenges, though some CSOs have since developed means of anonymous data sharing in order to overcome these restrictions.[19] Though LGBTQ activism has been effectively banned following the November 2023 Russian Supreme Court decision, encrypted messaging apps like Telegram and Meta's online services (Instagram and Facebook), blocked in Russia in March 2022 but accessible via virtual private network (VPN), play a significant role in enabling communication between the remaining LGBTQ-focused CSOs, grassroots initiatives, and community members, in addition to helping disseminate information related to emigration, especially those most affected by Russia's 2022 invasion of Ukraine. Another significant development in this most recent chapter of state persecution is the propagation of virtual help bots, designed by CSOs to address specific instances of psychological and legal help for individuals in need of immediate anonymous assistance.[20] Across countries such as Georgia, Türkiye, Armenia, Poland, and Germany, support networks for non-heterosexual Russian speakers have proliferated, designed to offer refuge, including temporary housing, immigration assistance, community support, language learning, and cultural enrichment.[21] As discussed in Chapter 7, these initiatives in the face of exceedingly stringent state prosecution exemplify the strength and fortitude of Russian LGBTQ persons to continue to assist their communities and offer support, whether legal, psychological, or emotional, to those who most need it.

As was done for the other countries, we analyzed the frequency and content of posts on X (formerly Twitter) relating to the Russian LGBTQ presence online. Due to many of the factors described above, such as online censorship related to the "gay propaganda law", subsequent legislation, and the popularity of encrypted messaging apps, our findings are less revealing than those of our other cases. Language also plays a role. The intersection of English-language Queer Theory and decoloniality aligns in the Russian case. While the term 'queer' (*kvir*), has gained in-community popularity, other sexual identity categories such as 'gay' (*gei*) or 'lesbian' (*lesbyanka*) are more frequently used.[22] The usage of 'LGBT' (RU/UKR: ЛГБТ) defies this trend, likely due to the term's increasing international usage (see Bar Chart 8.1).

Russia

Frequencies of LGBTQ related terms

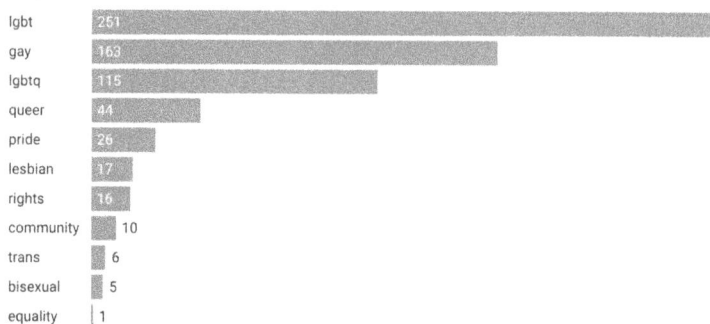

lgbt	251
gay	163
lgbtq	115
queer	44
pride	26
lesbian	17
rights	16
community	10
trans	6
bisexual	5
equality	1

Created with Datawrapper

Bar Chart 8.1   Data illustrating frequencies of LGBTQ-related terms in Russia.

Examining tweet frequencies over time reveals recurring spikes that align with particular events or surges in discussion. Keywords, particularly 'LGBT' (ЛГБТ), are prominent in these conversations, and tweets with high engagement demonstrate the audience's strong interest in these topics. We tracked tweet frequencies for the period from 2023 to 2024, as shown in (Bar Chart 8.1). The most visible peak in the graph, for instance, occurred during June 2023, or the final LGBTQ Pride Month prior to a rash of legislation banning gender-affirming care the following month, and the labeling of the 'international LGBT movement' as 'extremist' in November 2023, effectively banning all forms of queer activism. Another relatively popular post celebrated the resistance of the Kazakh government to undertake a similar 'gay propaganda law' as has taken effect in Russia (Graph 8.4).

LGBTQ-Related Themes Across Cases

The analysis of LGBTQ-related tweets from the MENA region, Singapore, and Russia reveals distinct thematic focuses, reflecting the unique sociopolitical and cultural contexts of each region (see Bar Charts 8.1–8.3). In the MENA region, the discourse is heavily centered around "pride" and "community," with these terms being the most frequently mentioned. This indicates a significant emphasis on LGBTQ visibility and solidarity within the community. The frequent use of "rights" and "equality" suggests an ongoing struggle for legal recognition and social acceptance. The relatively lower occurrences of terms like "gay," "lesbian," and "trans" might reflect a broader and less specific discourse on LGBTQ issues, possibly due to the region's generally conservative stance on these topics. In Russia, the term "lgbt" is the most

Views per tweet (2023-24)

Search data retrieved from social media platform X using hashtags used by LGBTQ communities

Russia

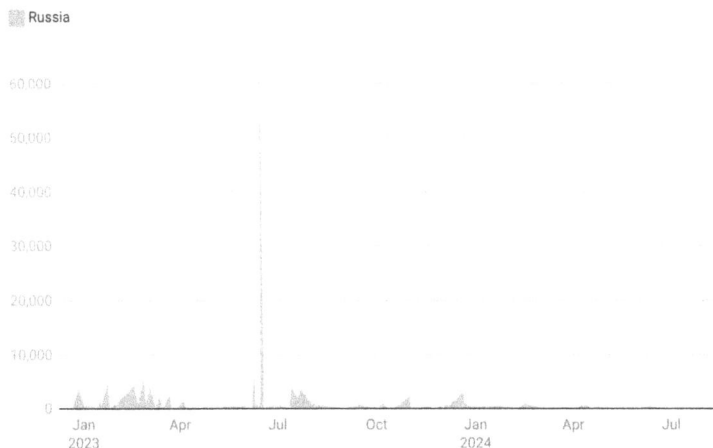

To protect privacy of users hashtags are not disclosed.
Chart created by the authors • Source: X • Created with Datawrapper

Graph 8.4 Chart with data on tweet views in Russia.

MENA region

Frequencies of LGBTQ related terms

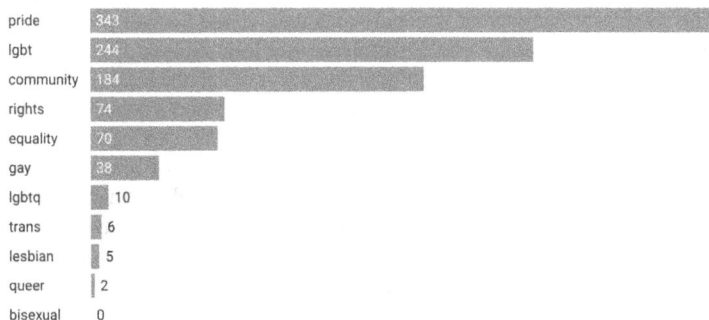

pride	343
lgbt	244
community	184
rights	74
equality	70
gay	38
lgbtq	10
trans	6
lesbian	5
queer	2
bisexual	0

Chart by the authors • Source: X • Created with Datawrapper

Bar Chart 8.2 Data illustrating frequencies of LGBTQ-related terms in the MENA region.

Singapore

Frequencies of LGBTQ related terms

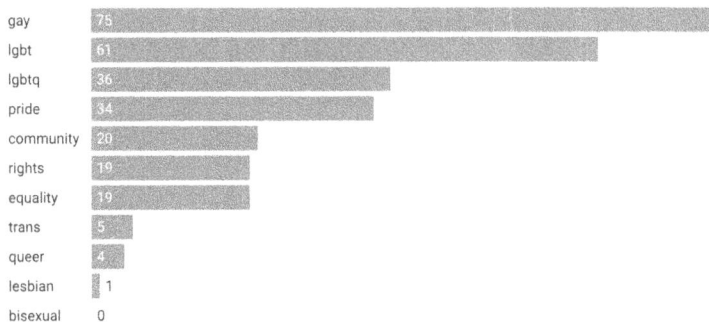

gay	75
lgbt	61
lgbtq	36
pride	34
community	20
rights	19
equality	19
trans	5
queer	4
lesbian	1
bisexual	0

Created with Datawrapper

Bar Chart 8.3 Data illustrating frequencies of LGBTQ-related terms in Singapore.

frequent, followed by 'gay" and "lgbtq," highlighting a strong focus on LGBTQ identity and related challenges. The prominence of "queer" and "pride" underscores the community's efforts to assert their identities and celebrate diversity despite the restrictive legal environment. The lower frequency of "rights" and "equality" compared to identity-focused terms suggests that the discourse may be more about visibility and existence rather than specific legal battles. This aligns with Russia's harsh stance on LGBTQ rights, where activism often faces significant legal and societal obstacles. Singapore presents a unique case where the term "gay" is the most frequent, followed closely by "lgbt" and "lgbtq." This indicates a strong focus on gay rights, possibly linked to the campaign against Section 377A, which criminalizes sex between men. The significant presence of "pride," "community," and "equality" reflects a robust movement toward social acceptance and legal reform. The relatively high frequency of terms related to specific identities and the legal framework suggests a more organized and targeted advocacy effort compared to the MENA and Russia. Overall, the analysis highlights the varying stages and focuses of LGBTQ advocacy in these regions. While the MENA region emphasizes community and pride amidst broader human rights struggles, Russia's discourse is dominated by identity assertion in a repressive environment. Singapore, on the other hand, shows a more structured approach towards legal reform and social acceptance, reflecting its unique sociopolitical landscape.

Conclusion

This chapter provided a meta-analysis of diverse and often subversive activities undertaken by LGBTQ advocates within repressive sociopolitical and cultural contexts. By examining a variety of case studies and utilizing various data visualization tools, we captured the daily struggles and resilience strategies of LGBTQ communities across different regions. Our analysis extends the discussions from earlier chapters, particularly the critical examination of repressive political strategies in Russia and Poland, and offers a broader, transversal view of collective action and contentious politics. Our investigation into the evolving public opinion and legal frameworks in regions like the MENA, Singapore, and Russia has highlighted the complex interplay between grassroots advocacy and institutional reform. The visualizations created through textual visualization tools have not only contextualized these struggles but also provided valuable insights into how geographical and sociopolitical contexts shape LGBTQ activism and community building. However, rather than offering a universal blueprint, this chapter highlights the significance of adopting a cross-disciplinary and intersectional approach to comprehend and support LGBTQ movements. The presented typology of subversive activities and strategies acts as an essential roadmap for researchers, advocates, and students, inspiring further inquiry in these crucial areas. By illuminating the resilience and adaptability of queer communities, this chapter aided the ongoing struggle for equality and justice, stressing the necessity for sustained, nuanced analysis and advocacy across various sociopolitical contexts.

Notes

1 See website at https://www.queeringthemap.com/, accessed 17 July 2024.
2 See website at https://www.nyclgbtsites.org/, accessed 17 July 2024.
3 See website at https://lbs.wustl.edu/mapping-lgbtq-st-louis, accessed 17 July 2024.
4 See website at https://www.queersacramento.com/, accessed 17 July 2024.
5 See website at https://www.mappingthegayguides.org, accessed 17 July 2024.
6 See website at https://outhistory.org/, accessed 17 July 2024.
7 See website at https://octoparse.com, accessed 31 July 2024.
8 See website at https://voyant-tools.org, accessed 31 July 2024.
9 See website at https://www.equaldex.com, accessed 30 July 2024.
10 See website at https://www.equaldex.com/compare/jordan/united-arab-emirates, accessed 30 July 2024.
11 See website at https://www.equaldex.com/compare/jordan/united-arab-emirates, accessed 30 July 2024.
12 See website at https://www.equaldex.com/compare/armenia/saudi-arabia, accessed 30 July 2024.
13 For more detailed and specific data, visit Equaldex's comparison pages and their public opinion surveys section: https://www.equaldex.com/surveys, https://www.equaldex.com/compare/jordan/united-arab-emirates, https://www.equaldex.com/compare/armenia/saudi-arabia, accessed 30 July 2024.
14 See website at https://www.equaldex.com/region/singapore, accessed 31 July 2024.
15 See website at https://www.equaldex.com/region/russia, accessed 2 August 2024.
16 See website at https://www.equaldex.com/region/russia, accessed 2 August 2024.
17 See Human Rights Watch, "Russia: New Anti-Gay Crackdown in Chechnya," *Human Rights Watch*, accessed from: https://www.hrw.org/news/2019/05/08/russia-new-anti-gay-crackdown-chechnya?gad_source=1&gclid=CjwKCAjwk8e1BhAL EiwAc8MHiChaAXumm63JNB9f8RyRs7naaMjPaFnegzt2xgXdCfO9a8aqBWFD xRoC11EQAvD_BwE

18 See Alexander Sasha Kondakov, *Violent Affections: Queer Sexuality, Techniques of Power, and Law in Russia,* (London: University College London Press, 2022).
19 See, for example, the most recent schedule of the Moscow Community Center for LGBT+ Initiatives (MCC), accessible at https://docs.google.com/spreadsheets/d/1OhNaAlf-KH08QsNqCrZzmQo9ZBJ4V8zxJv2Na2Ot6Nc/edit?gid=13218173 76#gid=1321817376, accessed 3 August 2024.
20 See, for example, those offered by the Russian LGBT Network and the Sphere Foundation.
21 See, for example, The Ark (Kovcheg), accessed from: https://kovcheg.live/en/ark/.
22 For a discussion of the language of Queer Theory and its usage in Russia, see Alexander Sasha Kondakov, *Violent Affections: Queer Sexuality, Techniques of Power, and Law in Russia,* (London: University College London Press, 2022).

Reference

Ho, Tammy. 2024. "Growing Acceptance of LGBTQ+ Rights in Singapore, But Generational Divides Remain." Ipsos. June 10, 2024. https://www.ipsos.com/en-sg/growing-acceptance-lgbtq-rights-singapore-generational-divides-remain

Conclusion
Closing Reflections, Queer Research, and Climate Change

This book provided an overview of the multifaceted nature of LGBTQ activism and the rich tapestry of collaborations and initiatives taking place across different regions globally, particularly in non-Western contexts. Activist networks such as the SAYAN network in Asia and Adelante in Latin America mentioned in our introduction exemplify this burgeoning transnational cooperation. While these initiatives often receive financial support from Western partners like the European Union, there is a growing movement within these regions to develop unique, locally tailored strategies that challenge the dominance of Western-centric LGBTQ discourses, sometimes referred to as the "gay international" (Massad 2007). This development is significant not only for its immediate impact on LGBTQ rights but also for its broader implications in the field of postcolonial queer studies. It highlights the need to reframe discussions around LGBTQ issues to include diverse geographic and cultural perspectives, particularly in light of rising illiberalism and homophobia in certain regions. Our book aimed at contributing to this discourse by providing empirical evidence through a series of case studies that explore these dynamics in various global contexts.

As emphasized at the beginning of our book, the handful of selected case studies we included in our book do not render justice to the heterogenous layers and manifestations of LGBTQ communities broadly, as we recognize these communities as social constructs with real-life implications. Identity formation is crucial, particularly for sexual minorities who navigate changing social, political, and cultural landscapes. Yet, with our book, we intended to delve into these complexities, offering insights into the nuances, challenges, and tensions within larger LGBTQ groups. Our exploration was grounded in spatial theory, drawing from the concepts of Bourdieu and Foucault to provide a rich understanding of how sexual minorities engage in diverse settings. Our research also employed a critical perspective, examining emerging and alternative spaces for LGBTQ emancipation against a backdrop of global uncertainties, such as illiberal political trends, ecological crises, and regional conflicts. These factors have impacted the development of queer spaces, especially in regions where diverse LGBTQ communities are less established.

DOI: 10.4324/9781003565871-13

By leveraging spatial theory, we sought to map and provide a conceptual framework of these practices and trends, contributing to a comprehensive understanding of how sexual minorities navigate these complex environments. Our book also explored the intersection of LGBTQ issues with broader socioeconomic and developmental challenges. It thus provided a critical and comprehensive examination of LGBTQ activism and community building across different regions, emphasizing the need for context-specific approaches and the importance of ethical research practices. It seeks to enrich the field of queer studies by offering new perspectives on the challenges and opportunities faced by LGBTQ communities worldwide, against the backdrop of global uncertainties and postcolonial legacies.

In Chapter 1, we highlighted the conceptual and methodological barriers in queer studies, emphasizing the importance of spatial theory in understanding the challenges faced by LGBTQ communities amidst global uncertainties. It scrutinizes contemporary queer literature and the impact of postcolonial legacies and cultural polarization on queer activism. Chapter 2 employed a mixed-method approach, using qualitative analysis and digital visualization to map the practices of LGBTQ communities. It highlighted the synergies among community members across different regions, addressing the challenges associated with cartographic research. It proposes a roadmap for capturing the evolution of cross-regional dynamics and the emancipatory power of online communities. The creation of alternative spaces for sexual minorities during political transitions is featured front and center in Chapter 3. Using Foucauldian concepts of heterotopia, we examined how social media and collective action create fragile spatialities for LGBTQ activism in the face of secularist and Islamist traditions. Drawing on diverse sources to analyze discursive patterns and public debates within Lebanese and Tunisian societies, Chapter 4 expanded on these conceptual frameworks scrutinizing how art and social media facilitate the creation of spaces for LGBTQ minorities. We demonstrated the relationship between queer activism and democratization, showing how activism adapts during periods of political reform stagnation. In Chapter 5 we continued our examination of LGBTQ advocacy in restrictive environments, shifting to Asia. We discussed the non-confrontational modes of activism in Singapore, where pragmatic values shape the perception and protection of individual rights. Through narrative interviews with local activists, the chapter explores how these modes of advocacy are conducted and how activists define themselves amidst cultural polarization. Chapter 6 then investigated queer activism in illiberal contexts, focusing on Poland. The chapter analyzed the impact of Europeanization and the cultural-religious opposition on LGBTQ activities. It also examined the influence of student activism and the cultivation of refugee spaces, considering Poland's position as a destination for LGBTQ minorities from former communist states. The chapter concluded with an overview of the changing political landscape following the 2023 parliamentary election. In our Chapter 7, we dove into the repressive politics of autocratic regimes, using Russia as a case study. We looked at how the Russian government uses scapegoating campaigns against LGBTQ communities to distract from regime threats. The chapter mapped the conditions and responses of advocacy groups amidst increased persecution and state-condoned violence. Chapter 8 expanded on the methodological nuts and bolts presented in Chapter 2 and provided a meta-analysis of the issues discussed in the book. It showed how LGBTQ communities adapt to societal and political challenges by drawing on subversive tools and activities in repressive socio-political and cultural contexts to coexist and promote their cause, if possible. The chapter offered a holistic framework built on case studies to understand the daily struggles of LGBTQ community members across various regions. It aimed to inspire further research with a cross-disciplinary, intersectional perspective. Overall, our book offered a rich and nuanced exploration of LGBTQ activism across different global contexts, emphasizing the importance of spatial theory, digital visualization, and intersectional analysis in understanding the complexities of queer communities' struggles and emancipatory practices.

Queer Studies, the Research Road Ahead, and the Issue of Climate Change

Given our global approach, we are nonetheless aware of remaining challenges and shortcomings. Our analysis is constrained by a limited number of case studies, which may not fully capture the diverse experiences and strategies of LGBTQ activism worldwide. Additionally, incorporating more interview data from a broader range of case studies could enhance the narrative style of storytelling, providing a more in-depth and personal perspective on the lived experiences of activists. Another significant area for improvement is the creation of crowdsourced virtual maps. These maps could highlight additional trends and emerging patterns across different regions and LGBTQ communities, offering a dynamic and interactive tool for researchers, activists, and policymakers. By addressing these challenges, future research could provide a more comprehensive and inclusive understanding of LGBTQ activism, enriching the current theoretical frameworks and practical approaches discussed in the book.

Our ongoing project continues to complete the existing data, further integrating interview data from community members across different regions and creating narrative-style storytelling that is embedded in the virtual, online maps. As such, the goal is to create a living online documentation platform that is publicly available, and which continues to tell the story of important strides to tackle injustice and marginalization of lesser visible groups and individuals from a transnational and cross-regional perspective. Despite remaining challenges and obstacles, including notably the safety and well-being of LGBTQ community members, current and past engagements and activities have proven that the time is in favor of transformative change, including research, the harnessing of online spaces and the continued collaboration of stakeholders across professions and disciplines.

In conclusion, we shift our focus to a pressing but under-explored thematic issue in view of global queer studies: the linkage between LGBTQ and climate change risks. Drawing on Elizabeth Weinberg's 2022 book *Unsettling: Surviving Extinction Together*, Emilie Kostecka reflects on the intersection of environmental issues with capitalist concepts, heteronormativity and racism and further drawing out the role of queerness in this context (Kostecka 2023; see also Bauman 2018; Weber 2016). While her thoughts integrate Weinberg's intersectional approach and grounded critique of some of the core issues of climate change, others have examined the (in)visibility of different queer communities, notably in terms of climate change impacts and risks (Dalton 2023; Goldsmith, Raditz, and Méndez 2022; Kilpatrick et al. 2023). In the United States, for instance, where members of different LGBTQ communities are more visible and have a stronger voice than in more repressive contexts and countries where queerness remains relatively invisible in the public eye, the burden carried by members of these communities is especially heavy. As Leo Goldsmith and Michelle Bell show, LGBTQ populations face significant institutional discrimination in housing, employment, and healthcare due to federal and state policies, which negatively affect their ability to respond to environmental hazards (Goldsmith and Michelle 2022). These social determinants of health are linked to unequal environmental exposures, resulting in higher rates of chronic diseases like respiratory and cardiovascular illnesses and cancer in LGBTQ communities compared to cisgender, heterosexual individuals. Goldsmith and Bell thus underline how environmental exposures disproportionately impact LGBTQ populations, providing examples and discussing the role of social institutions in influencing resilience to these environmental stressors (Goldsmith and Michelle 2022).

These closing thoughts underscore the need for a more transversal and holistic approach when addressing climate change risks in view of different queer communities across transnational and cross-regional contexts, and we therefore urge stakeholders, advocates and policymakers to embrace an intersectional perspective to fuel integral responses to the myriad existing challenges and impeding climate risks ahead of us.

References

Bauman, Whitney A. 2018. "Queer Values for a Queer Climate: Developing a Versatile Planetary Ethic." In *Meaningful Flesh: Reflections on Religion and Nature for a Queer Planet*, 103–124. Santa Barbara: Punctum Books.

Dalton, Drew. 2023. "Have We Left Behind the Rainbow Warriors? The Climate Emergency and Its Impact on Global Queer People and Their Communities." In *Gender, Sexuality and the UN's SDGs: A Multidisciplinary Approach*, edited by Drew Dalton and Angela Smith, 17–40. Cham: Springer International Publishing.

Goldsmith, Leo, and Michelle L. Bell. 2022. "Queering Environmental Justice: Unequal Environmental Health Burden on the LGBTQ+ Community." *American Journal of Public Health* 112 (1): 79–87.

Goldsmith, Leo, Vanessa Raditz, and Michael Méndez. 2022. "Queer and Present Danger: Understanding the Disparate Impacts of Disasters on LGBTQ+ Communities."
Disasters 46 (4): 946–73.

Kilpatrick, Claire, Kieran Higgins, Seth Atkin, and Stephan Dahl. 2023. "A Rapid Review of the Impacts of Climate Change on the Queer Community." *Environmental
Justice*, July. https://doi.org/10.1089/env.2023.0010

Kostecka, Emilie A. 2023. "Queerness in the Age of Surviving Climate Change." *Parks
Stewardship Forum* 39 (2). https://doi.org/10.5070/P539260967.

Massad, Joseph. 2007. *Desiring Arabs*. Chicago, IL: University of Chicago Press.

Weber, Cynthia. 2016. *Queer International Relations*. Oxford Studies in Gender and
International Relations. New York: Oxford University Press.

Index

Note: Locators in *italics* represent figures and locators followed by "n" refer to end notes.

For Product Safety Concerns and Information please contact our EU representative GPSR@taylorandfrancis.com
Taylor & Francis Verlag GmbH, Kaufingerstraße 24, 80331 München, Germany